Carry on, Understudies

The Author

Michelene Wandor is a poet, playwright and critic. She was Poetry Editor and a regular theatre reviewer for *Time Out* magazine (1971–82), and she has written extensively for and about theatre and radio in Britain. Her own plays for theatre are published in *Five Plays* (Playbooks/Journeyman, 1984), and her prolific work for radio includes dramatisations of H. G. Wells's *Kipps* (runner-up for the Sony Drama Awards, 1985) and an eight-part serial of Dostoyevsky's *The Brothers Karamazov*. Her poetry books include *Upbeat* (1982) and *Gardens of Eden* (1984). As editor she has produced *On Gender and Writing* (Pandora, 1983) and four volumes of *Plays by Women* (Methuen). She is the author of *Look Back in Gender: sexuality and the family in post-war British drama* (Methuen, 1987), and her prose fiction is collected in *Guests in the Body* (Virago, 1986). She gives regular talks about theatre, poetry readings, and runs play-writing workshops at various places, including the Guildhall School of Music and Drama in London.

Extracts from press reviews

'A direct and provocative investigation into sexual politics in the British theatre, particularly during the 1970s ... Michelene Wandor has made a radical analysis without appearing aesthetically raw or politically simple.' – Catherine Paice, *Plays and Players*.

'This excellent book ... recognizes that theatre is a barometer of the social climate and shows how the battles that have raged around sexuality throughout this century have been reflected on its stage ... It's a must. Buy it.' – Noel Greig, *Gay News*

' ... certainly packs a punch. Not only is it an analysis of sexual politics in modern theatre, but it also serves as a history of feminist and gay theatre over the last thirteen years.' – Sarah Dunant, *Spare Rib*

'It provides a first and essential feminist overview of theatrical developments that are enormously influential in British theatre ... accessible, lucid and a much-needed mapping of hitherto uncharted territory.' – Frances Rifkin, *Equity Journal*

'Should be on the reference and current reading shelf of every critic, reviewer and drama teacher throughout the country.' – Peggy Kessel, *Comment*

Carry on, Understudies
Theatre and Sexual Politics

Michelene Wandor

Routledge & Kegan Paul
London and New York

Original edition first published in 1981
by Eyre Methuen Ltd as Understudies
This edition first published in 1986
by Routledge & Kegan Paul plc

11 New Fetter Lane, London EC4P 4EE

Published in the USA by
Routledge & Kegan Paul Inc.
in association with Methuen Inc.
29 West 35th Street, New York, NY 10001

Set in Sabon 10 on 12 pt
by Input Typesetting Ltd, London
and printed in Great Britain
by The Guernsey Press Co Ltd
Guernsey, Channel Islands

Library of Congress Cataloging in Publication Data

Wandor, Michelene.

Carry on understudies.

Bibliography: p.
Includes index.
1. Women in the theater——England.   2. Feminist
theater——England.   3. Theater——Great Britain—History—
20th century   4. Theater——Political aspects.
5. English drama——Women authors——History and criticism.
6. English drama—20th century—History and criticism.
I. Title.
PN2595.13.W65W36   1986   792'.09'09352042   85–30117

British Library CIP data also available

ISBN 0–7102–0817–0 (c)
      0–7102–0937–1 (pb)

Contents

vi *Contents*

Curtain-raiser

Mankind (sic) always sets itself only such problems as it can solve; for when we look closer we will always find that the problem itself only arises when the material conditions for its solution are already present or at least in process of coming into being.

(Karl Marx, Preface to *A Contribution to the Critique of Political Economy*, 1859)

ALICK. What is charm exactly, Maggie?
MAGGIE. Oh, it's – it's a sort of bloom on a woman. If you have it, you don't need to have anything else; and if you don't have it, it doesn't much matter what else you have. Some women, the few, have charm for all; and most have charm for one. But some have charm for none.

(J. M. Barrie, *What Every Woman Knows*, 1908)

What has poor woman done that she must be
Debarr'd from sense and sacred poetry?
Why in this age has Heaven allow'd you more,
And Woman less of wit than heretofore?
We once were famed in story, and could write
Equal to men; cou'd govern, nay, could fight.
We still have passive valour, and can show,
Wou'd custom give us leave, the active too,
Since we no provocation want from you.

(Epilogue to _Sir Patient Fancy_, by Aphra Behn,
1677)

That's Entertainment

The queen who's grotesquely obscene
Or the dyke who is out for a fight,
Butch or fem, he-women, she-men:
That's entertainment?

The crowd's guaranteed to laugh loud
When it hears any jokes about queers,
Yes, we're good – good targets for mud,
That's entertainment.

It may be you've seen how we're shown on the screen,
A dyke's sister George and she's a has-been.
Ev'ry Boy in the Band is a queen; did you see Sebastiane?
It's all cock and blarney.

And so, now where do we go?
Do we take this image, this fake?
Or do we say it's good to be gay!
It's we who have to pay, so let's all shout for gay,
Gay Entertainment.
  (From *Jingle Ball*, Gay Sweatshop, 1976, lyrics by Drew
                                            Griffiths)

Preface to the second edition

This book is a revised, updated and greatly expanded edition of a monograph first published in 1981. The original book came into being after I had suggested to Methuen a book, edited by myself, of three of the collaboratively written plays about sexual politics, from the early to middle 1970s. The editor did not feel that the plays were 'good' enough as plays to warrant publishing; we then had a rather tetchy, not to say argumentative, telephone conversation, in which I said how important it was to document such theatre work, that it had particular merits in its own right, and that there was enough happening which I could write a book about, but what was the point of writing a book about work which would never see the light of print? The conversation ended in great disappointment and frustration on my part; but about a week later I had a letter from Methuen's editor, taking me up on my 'suggestion' to write a book. After some thought, I decided to go ahead – such offers do not come by every post – and over the next few months began work on what was to become *Understudies*, while also finding a publisher for the anthology of plays.[1]

Understudies took me two years to write – 1978–80. The entire book was based on original research, in the sense that no plays were in print, and apart from a very small number of articles and reviews, there was no secondary source material. I had myself been writing plays and writing theatre reviews for *Time Out*, and during the 1970s had seen pretty well 100 per cent of all the plays I documented and discussed. I collected about a hundred hours of interview material, talking to people all over the country. I drew very heavily and thankfully on the general socialist criticism which was being written and discussed in study groups throughout the 1970s; Marx, Althusser, Lukács, Goldman *et al.* were added to my conventional, immensely useful from a literary point of view, Leavisite Eng. Lit. education. I was also involved as one of many participants in a thoroughgoing commitment to the theatre work which the fringe was developing – the 'fringe', the 'alternative theatre', 'political' theatre – all dynamic and exploratory areas of work, where my own plays had been produced. I followed and took part in the discussions about subsidised versus co-opted theatre; argued about whether or not writing for television meant that writers had 'sold out', or were fighting the good fight in their own way. The tone of the first *Understudies* was a matter of great struggle for me to define: I wanted to reflect both the intellectual rigour of the theory with which I was engaging, and also the immediate, almost evangelical, certainly polemical, excitement which accompanied the public appearance of what later came to be called 'feminist' or 'women's theatre', and 'gay theatre'.

I was also very aware indeed that I was being put in the position of implicitly having to 'justify' the importance of this new strand of alternative theatre which, like all theatre, is dependent on audiences to keep going, and which needed to be described and documented as well as treated critically. In the event I held back on criticism at the time, in the interests of writing an only partly critical documentary.

During the years that followed the publication of the book, a number of things happened. Because it did so well initially in terms of sales for the kind of book it was, when I returned to my original suggestion of an anthology, it was taken up in a form which backed up and complemented *Understudies*. The idea was to edit an annual anthology of plays by contemporary women writers, and to date there have been four such anthologies published by Methuen, each containing four plays. These books too have done well (they are incredibly good value for money), and together with *Understudies* have helped theatres, companies and students interested in good plays by women writers, and have taken their place on 'women and theatre' drama courses in colleges and universities all over the country.

However, despite *Understudies'* relative success, after various discussions over the years about revising and updating it, in the event, Methuen in their wisdom (or lack of it?) finally decided to let it go out of print. I have nothing but gratitude for the intelligence and extremely astute publishing sense of Routledge editor Philippa Brewster in taking on the book, and allowing me to update it, and, what is just as important, to expand it so that it is a more critical book as well.

In the revision, virtually no page has been untouched by my brain and typewriter. Lazy sentences have been tightened; additional information included; political and aesthetic ideas developed; the place of women in the theatre industry has been more fully discussed; and there is now a far longer section at the end which discusses the work of women playwrights, many of whom had not begun writing, or only just, when the first version of the book was published.

Carry On, Understudies remains a critical history of the relationship between theatre, class and gender; it is about feminism, women and gays, and the representation of sexuality in theatre during the 1970s and the first half of the 1980s. It places those fifteen years in their social, historical, political and theatrical context (perhaps the shortest 'history of the world' ever written!) and it aims to cut a rigorous swathe through the idiomatic catchphrases of 'feminist theatre', 'women's theatre', 'gay theatre' in a way that will be useful to academics, students, theatre practitioners, critics and audiences. In other words, it is for anyone who is concerned about the future of the theatre, and the way it represents half the population (women), half its audiences (women) and aspects of homosexuality which have hitherto been suppressed or distorted.

Some things have changed since I first began drawing this material together in 1978: a handful of women playwrights are now in the public eye, with challenging, successful plays. The fringe is no longer new, and has its own histories. More women working in the theatre are less content with the opportunities offered them. But there is still a very long way to go before women are 50 per cent of the theatre workforce, and before the full range of all sexual choices is represented in the content of plays. The theatre still needs sexual politics.

Michelene Wandor, June 1985

Acknowledgments

I would like to thank all the groups and individuals who gave their time to talk to me in 1979–80 for the first version of this book. Unless a source is given, all quotations are from interviews conducted by the author in 1979 for the purpose of this book. The first version was dedicated 'to everyone who is concerned about the future of theatre'. This revised, expanded and updated edition is particularly dedicated to the memory of two people who are no longer alive to see the results of their own pioneering work: Verity Bargate, who for so many years did so much to encourage new writing at the Soho Poly theatre, and gave particular support to women writers, and Drew Griffiths, writer, performer, director, and one of the founders of Gay Sweatshop. They are both sadly missed.

Introduction to the first edition

This book is about the relationship between sexual politics and the alternative theatre of the 1970s and the first half of the 1980s. This strand of theatre has its roots in the very varied touring companies, arts venues and individuals who have exposed, in their work, the axiomatic link between politics and art. They vary in the forms, ideologies and aims of their work; they range from the openly, polemically agitprop to the surrealist and the expressionist; but they share one common intention: in different ways they have sought to democratise the social division of labour in the theatre by developing flexible and collaborative work methods, by introducing theatre to new audiences, and by representing the experiences and interests of groups of oppressed and exploited people.

The alternative theatre has raised important questions about the way theatre is organised, produced and distributed. Sexual politics introduced another kind of radical critique to its vocabulary by raising questions about a division of labour based on gender, and about distorted and debasing representations of sexuality. The theatre industry, like other cultural industries, operates through a hierarchical structure, in which artistic and administrative decisions are largely in the hands of men. This situation exists not as a result of a massive and conscious conspiracy among men to put women down, but as a far more complex consequence (part conscious, part unconscious) of received assumptions about relations among and between the sexes, based on an ideology which assumes that the biological differences between men and women must necessarily mean that their fields of social activity must be different, and that men's work is socially more important than women's work.

Such an ideology pervades our society; it has been analysed and combated by the new wave of Western feminism which began in the late 1960s. This feminist movement, more far-reaching than its suffragette precursor, has, at its most radical, approached the social and sexual divisions within our society by analysing them from the point of view of women. This has produced an analysis of the repressive aspects of sexuality and the family, initiating a reassessment of the social roles of men and women, and a more open attitude to sexuality – homosexuality as well as heterosexuality. Feminist and gay activism has had great cultural impact in theatre work – overwhelmingly unpublished, only occasionally documented and reviewed, but of fundamental importance to theatre as a whole – from improving the position of women as workers, to changing the way women are represented in plays, and to consolidating an experimental theatre movement which challenges the repressive aspects of the sexual and the social division of labour. This book, then, is about the relationship between theatre, class and gender. This makes it partisan towards the work of women and gays, particularly when it has been spurred by feminist or by a politicised gay consciousness.

The book is also partisan in that it is written by someone who is a practitioner on both sides of the theatrical fence: I have been a playwright since 1970, and have reviewed and written articles about theatre since 1971. This has enabled me to write 'from the inside' to some degree, knowing and having worked with many of the people mentioned in the book, and being familiar with many of the debates and differences in a varied, political theatre movement. Because I live and work in London I have concentrated on work done in London mainly by white theatre workers and on groups and individuals who are likely to be more widely known in alternative theatre than to a general readership. The book aims to document work in a way which will be constructive to those already familiar with it, to explain the importance of this work to people unfamiliar with or hostile to it, and to raise some fundamental questions about theatre today.

The relationship between sexual politics and theatre has its roots before the watershed year of 1968. It also has repercussions in the way women and sexuality are represented in radio, television and film. At the moment theatre is the medium in which most experimental work has been done. It is only by understanding the context and process of this experimentation that we can make sense of the plays it produces and evaluate them. The opening chapter presents a summary of the historical, political and aesthetic context in which feminist and gay theatre happens. It is necessarily highly schematised but it indicates the complexity of approach which is ultimately necessary in order to understand the relationship between theatre and sexual politics.

The bulk of the book concentrates on the most important phases in sexual political theatre, with particular emphasis on their moments of origin. I have chosen to concentrate on origins and analyse tendencies rather than attempt a comprehensive, archival note on every play that might be of interest. There can be very few people working in the theatre who are totally ignorant of the way in which the position of women and assumptions about sexuality are changing, but there are still too few who have either the confidence or the commitment to take an active part in those changes. I hope this book will help increase that number.

Michelene Wandor, 1981

1
Contexts

Early political theatre and feminism

Theatre and performance skills of all kinds have always played a role during periods of social and political change in Britain. Emerging political movements have used theatre and music to express and support their struggles, and radical social change has also affected the avant-garde wings of theatre, which are always receptive to new ideas. During the 1840s plays were performed in support of the Chartists, and in the course of the nineteenth century various attempts were made in London to establish theatres and produce plays for 'worker-audiences'.

Towards the end of the nineteenth century, with the founding of the Independent Labour Party and the Co-operative Movement, the influence of socially conscious playwrights, such as Ibsen and Shaw, took root in a climate of radical debate in Britain. Political activists drew sustenance as well as entertainment from the work of such playwrights. Eleanor Marx translated the first English version of Ibsen's play, *An Enemy of the People*, in 1888 (published in 1890). In 1885 she had taken part in a reading of *The Doll's House*, together with Edward Aveling and George Bernard Shaw. Although there is still a strong tendency in this country to pretend that 'art' and 'politics' have little or nothing to do with one another (or should have little or nothing . . .), there is an enormous amount of evidence to show how theatre is continually influenced by the new political ideas of its time.

In the early years of the twentieth century a National Association of Clarion Clubs (associated with *The Clarion* newspaper) put on plays with socialist and labour themes. The Workers' Theatre Movement (WTM, 1928–36) directed its attention to the rapidly changing political situation since the First World War. Receptive to cultural and political influences from Germany and the Soviet Union in particular, it introduced the agitprop montage form into British theatre, drawing on indigenous popular forms – sketches, music-hall, cabaret – harnessing theatre as a direct adjunct to the class struggle (for instance, during the General Strike of 1926).

The WTM was essentially an amateur theatre project; in 1936, when Unity Theatre was founded, the contribution of professional theatre workers politicised in particular by the anti-fascist movement, was an important factor. Unity's aim (shared with the New Theatre League) was to mobilise a united front of progressive theatre workers, just as the Left Book Club (started by publisher Victor Gollancz) and *Left Review* (a literary/political journal) did with writers and readers in the 1930s. In 1937 the Left Book Club started a Theatre Guild which by 1938 consisted of about 250 groups all over the country.

The growing agitation for women's suffrage in the second half of the nineteenth century, with its campaigns for women to be fully admitted into the professions, helped bring women more actively into radical theatre work. Many actresses were instrumental in producing and performing Ibsen's plays, both because of the ideas about women and independence with which he dealt, and because it gave them opportunities as actresses to play more challenging roles:

> What you won't be able to imagine . . . is the joy of having in our hands . . . such glorious actable stuff. If we had been thinking politically, concerning ourselves about the emancipation of women, we would not have given the Ibsen plays the kind of wholehearted enchanted devotion we did give. . . . Ibsen taught us something we were never to unlearn.
> (Actress Elizabeth Robins, quoted in Julie Holledge, *Innocent Flowers*, Virago, 1981)

In December 1908 the Actresses' Franchise League was formed, dedicated to supporting the struggle for female suffrage. At first they provided poems and monologues to entertain at political meetings, but soon began writing and producing short plays, as a way of contributing their professional talents to the cause. The plays were simple parables, based largely on the satirical, naturalistic sketch, but they are interesting because, although they mostly address themselves to showing how essential the vote is to women, they also reveal a broad grasp of the situation of women. The plays satirise what we would now call male chauvinism – crude male prejudice against women. They satirise the upper-class men and women who were against women's suffrage, and although often offering little more than a sophisticated version of the working-class stereotype, the plays do express sympathy with the plight of working-class women. In one play, *An Englishwoman's Home*, by a man, Arncliffe Sennet, men are wittily offered the franchise of sharing housework and childcare in return for the vote and the same work opportunities. The plays deal with the material conditions of women's lives, without much confrontation with psychological oppression, or sexual relationships. Three of these fascinating plays are included in Julie Holledge's excellent book *Innocent Flowers: Women in the Edwardian Theatre* (Virago, 1981).

Around 1913 the actresses turned their attention to conditions for women within the acting profession, beginning to campaign against its prejudices against women in certain jobs. An Independent Women's Theatre Company flourished briefly, but with the First World War and the muffling of suffragette militancy, this early feminist theatre largely faded from the public eye. During the 1920s and 1930s organised political feminism was far less visible; struggles to improve the position of women in society continued, but less publicly. Organisations continued to argue and work around specific issues, such as contraception and childcare, and within working-class organisations such as the Co-operative Guild feminism still found a presence. But theatre work controlled by women, and linking feminism and aesthetics, ceased to command its own space. There were a number of women who were very active within the Unity Theatre movement (such as sisters Angela and Joan Tuckett in Bristol) and there was the occasional play about the 'women's question' – equal rights for women, equal educational opportunities, abortion. But it was only well after the Second World War that feminism and theatre again came together;

this time in a greatly changed social and political situation in which radical post-war changes to the family had produced intense and contradictory pressures on women.

'Emancipation' and after

In 1928 women were finally granted the vote on the same terms as men. Many people assumed that the expression of women's needs and interests through the ballot box was therefore assured, but the historical and political complexity of social organisation is such that the freedom to vote is only one step along the way to self-determination. As Engels pointed out in his preface to *The Origin of the Family, Private Property and the State* (1884):

> The determining factor in history is, in the last resort, the production and reproduction of immediate life. But this itself is of a twofold character. On the one hand, the production of the means of subsistence, of food, clothing and shelter and the tools requisite therefore; on the other, the production of human beings themselves, the propagation of the species.

In today's advanced industrial society we take it for granted that these two forms of 'production' are separate: on the one hand the world of 'work' produces the material means of subsistence, and on the other is the 'family' – the centre of personal and emotional life. But the family is also in one sense a place where production of a fundamental and vital kind takes place – the production of human beings, and their reproduction (both biologically and socially) as the next generation of working people. Sociologist Ann Oakley has summarised the growing rift between paid work and the family as follows:

> 1) from 1750 until the early 1840s, when the family was increasingly displaced by the factory as the place of production, but women followed their traditional work out of the home; 2) from the 1840s until 1914, when a decline in the employment of married women outside the home was associated with the rising popularity of a belief in women's

natural domesticity; 3) from 1914 until the 1950s, when
there is a discernible, though uneven tendency towards the
growing employment of women, coupled with a retention of
housewifery as the primary role expected of all women.
(*Housewife*, Allen Lane, 1974, p. 34)

With the separation of productive work from the home and
family unit, the balance of relationships within the family shifted.
As the factory system replaced the family income with the man's
wage, the notion of man as sole breadwinner took on a material
reality. Working-class men were excluded more and more from a
practical share in running the home, while woman acquired a two-
fold responsibility: not only looking after home and children, but
also having to work outside the home with fewer job choices and
lower pay than men. At the same time, with the growing affluence
enjoyed by the expanding middle class, the situation of privileged
women narrowed down. For the Victorian patriarch, the idleness
of his women became a symbol of the extent of his wealth. The
image of the pale lady, languishing on her invalid bed, in semi-
darkness, protected from the harsh light of reality and society,
conveys perfectly the contradictory way in which the Victorian
middle-class woman was idealised. On the one hand she was
released from domestic drudgery by having servants; on the other
she was somehow forced to retreat into a twilight of invalidism to
give her any function at all. And as the gulf between rich and poor
widened, so did the gulf between men and women within each of
those two classes.

In the twentieth century, two world wars have ironically produced opportunities for women denied them during peacetime;
extra state support, job opportunities, education, welfare and nurseries have all been made available in the interests of the war
economy. After each war, many facilities were withdrawn, nurseries closed, and women were shunted back into the home to
'liberate' jobs for men, and to resume the task of rebuilding the
population. However, the 1944 Education Act consolidated and
advanced opportunities for higher education for both sexes, and
the third Labour government of 1945–51 launched a programme
of partial nationalisation and welfare reform. With the establishment of the Welfare State, it was widely assumed that the class

war was finally over. But although social benefits and growing national affluence improved the quality of life for most people, an oppressive social and sexual division of labour still existed, and new contradictions emerged:

> By the early fifties Keynesian capitalism had eliminated mass unemployment and allowed a steady increase in the material standard of living of the working class. It thereby appeared to annul the *positive* case for socialism that had been made for fifty years by the working-class movement: that capitalism was unable to prevent cyclical hunger and destitution. Simultaneously the Cold War allowed capitalist regimes everywhere to establish powerful *negative* identification of socialism with the political order of the Soviet Union under Stalin.
>
> (Perry Anderson, *New Left Review*, Jan.–Feb. 1965)

By the late 1950s the impact of the post-war boom was being felt: the expansion of the white-collar sector to service material expansion produced a new professional group. With the increase of material consumer goods developed a mass-distributed culture through TV, cinema and popular music. But the Campaign for Nuclear Disarmament (CND) and the university-based New Left, which both formed during this period, reflected a political concern for more than mere material improvement. CND, in its concern for a world threatened by the destructive aspects of nuclear power, drew into its membership working-class and lower-middle-class people in a new resurgence of political protest. The New Left initiated a revived interest in Marxist theory, and in Continental Marxist writing, as well as pinpointing the contradiction between the so-called liberal values of an affluent society with education available to all, and the realities of adult life in a society where young intellectual professionals were able to do little more than slot into a bureaucratised and technologised capitalism.

At the grassroots level of everyday and personal life, post-war society had a dramatic impact on the family; an extensive rehousing programme eroded the security of many working-class communities and attenuated family networks. The new technological consumer affluence brought many labour-saving devices for the housewife: vacuum cleaners, fridges, more efficient stoves, etc.; the matching advertising campaigns emphasised the self-sufficiency of each family unit; one of the effects of this was to isolate the woman at the centre of her individual family.

All these various changes produced new patterns of family life, with which sociologists and psychologists tried to deal throughout the 1950s and the 1960s. The reality was that large numbers of women still worked outside the home, but women's magazines extolled the virtues of feminine wife and mother, and domestic craft skills. In particular, graduate women were the object of a barrage from psychologists and the media on the ideals of wife and motherhood as an alternative 'career' for the educated woman, in which she not only nurtured her children in time-honoured fashion, but also acted as informal educator. At the same time new scientific advances – in particular improved forms of contraception – meant that women were no longer as tied to their childbearing function as their mothers had been. Whereas for men sexual pleasure and procreation had always been separate options, for the first time Western women were approaching a point where those options could be a reality for them too.

The material changes pressuring the family from outside, and the internal changes brought about by new conditions for women, were indirectly acknowledged in a number of legislative reforms passed by the Labour government during the second half of the 1960s. In 1967 an Abortion Act and an Act partially legalising male homosexuality were passed (female homosexuality has never been illegal – popular myth has it that when the first anti-homo-sexual legislation was passed in 1885, Queen Victoria was so horrified at the mere thought of lesbianism that she refused to believe it could exist, and hence it could not be made illegal . . .). In 1969 the Divorce Reform Act eased conditions for divorce, and in 1970 the Equal Pay Act proposed that equal pay for men and women should become a reality by the end of 1975. (It hasn't, unfortunately. Women's average earnings are still only about 70 per cent of men's average earnings.)

Although the State was indirectly responding to the changing conditions of family life, and although the problems were being aired in some areas – such as a running debate about the role of education for women – throughout the 1950s and early 1960s, all women were still being exhorted to find contentment in hearth and home. However, some people noticed and took the symptoms of growing female discontent seriously. In Britain sociologist Hannah Gavron conducted research on housebound working- and middle-class mothers in 1960–1; the results were published by Routledge & Kegan Paul and then Penguin in 1966 under the title of *The Captive Wife*. The book explored the problems of boredom, isolation and frustration experienced by women of both classes. In the United States journalist Betty Friedan wrote a book called *The Feminine Mystique*, published in 1962. Her book tackled the 'problem' of self-contained, suburban affluence more directly. Analysing and quoting from experiences of suburban housewives, she dissected the affluent American Dream as it turned into a nightmare for many of the women who had been expected (and who themselves expected) to find happiness and total fulfilment. She pinpointed the new symptoms of discontent, but could not yet identify the causes, nor, with any confidence, suggest a solution. For her the problem crystallised particularly around the fact that women were experiencing a very profound identity crisis. She called it 'the problem with no name'; it took the rest of the 1960s to be further identified, and it took the political and cultural watershed year of 1968 to supply a reservoir of activism from which theatre and feminism could draw new energy.

1968 – politics and theatre

During the early 1960s a restless youth movement, more affluent than their parents' generation, challenged the blandness of the dominant cultural offerings in television, cinema and popular music. Rock music, pop festivals, the 'underground' culture with its superficially 'permissive' attitudes to pleasure and sexuality (love and peace . . .) drew on the experiences of CND as well as exploiting the expansion of mass media such as the record industry. As world political events became more momentous (the Chinese cultural revolution in the mid-1960s, the American war in Vietnam, the invasion of Czechoslovakia and the French students' and workers' protest in 1968), increasing militancy from the working class, the New Left and the students resulted in a publicly visible renewal of class conflict and a socialist challenge to bourgeois ideology. The political and cultural exuberance of young people in 1968 drew attention to the passivity of the consumer alongside the exploitation of the worker, insisting that the day-to-day lives of ordinary people could be 'politicised' and changed, and that the quality of relationships between people was as important as greater material benefits. The bringing together of 'public' and 'private' concerns by a new generation of young socialists of different tendencies met the legislative liberalising (through reforms of laws dealing with the family and sexuality) of the 1960s.

The liberalisation of the State's attitude to divorce, certain aspects of sexuality and the family, and the new cultural lifestyles of the younger generation, were part of the climate in which theatre struggled for its own liberation from censorship. Theatre censorship had remained an anomaly among the arts. Films had to be scrutinised by censors in order to be given a certificate to be shown, but only after they were already made. Books could be prosecuted for being obscene (i.e. D. H. Lawrence's *Lady Chatterley's Lover* in 1960), but play manuscripts had to be submitted before production to the Lord Chamberlain, and could not go into rehearsal without his (sic) approval. He was empowered to demand changes in the text, and, as Kenneth Tynan pointed out in a beautifully turned article in the *Observer* (1965), combining wit with barely concealed fury:

> Since he is appointed directly by the sovereign, he is not responsible to the House of Commons. He inhabits a limbo aloof from democracy, answerable to his own hunches. The rules by which he judges plays are nowhere defined in law . . .

However, Tynan astutely summarised the way these unspoken and unwritten laws of censorship invariably worked in practice, on the real ideas and words in contemporary theatre:

> Since he is always recruited from the peerage, he naturally tends to forbid attacks on institutions like the Church and the Crown. He never permits plays about eminent British subjects, living or recently dead, no matter how harmless the content and despite the fact that Britain's libel laws are about the strictest on earth. Above all, he feels a paternal

need to protect his flock from exposure to words or gestures relating to bodily functions below the navel and above the upper thigh. This – the bedding-cum-liquid-and-solid-eliminating area – is what preoccupies him most, and involves the writers and producers who have to deal with him in the largest amount of wasted time.

(*A View of the English Stage*, Paladin, 1975)

It is interesting that in this somewhat satirical (but accurate) description, Tynan shows how censorship was applied to the most 'public' of subject matters (Church and Crown) and the most 'private' of bodily functions. Sexuality could not be represented in any way which was thought to violate ideas about 'public decency' and 'privacy'; love scenes (where they appeared) could not be acted on beds (the 'one foot on the floor' syndrome), if they were heterosexual; if they were homosexual, they had to be cut completely. Overt representations of, and references to, homosexuality were strictly taboo.

The actual process of submitting plays to the Lord Chamberlain was long and tedious. And once approved, a text could not be changed. Obviously this meant restrictions on subject matter, forms of imaginative expression, and the impossibility of very topical plays. Of course, theatre had always found ways round censorship (the proliferation of club theatres between the two world wars, for example), but as the 1960s progressed, the forces of liberalisation gained ground, and in 1968 the office of the Lord Chamberlain was finally abolished. Plays could now (in theory) be about anything, be topical, be subject to change from performance to performance, could include improvisation, and could match the needs of the theatre industry, within which there were changing attitudes to management, interest in new ways of working, and pressure to refocus the class content of many plays.

By the 1950s the influence of the actor/manager had virtually disappeared. In the early part of the 1950s a consortium of business and theatrical interests known as the 'Group' had initiated a series of West End plays which clung on to an increasingly outdated concept of the theatre-going public:

Many new plays seemed to be set in opulent houses in Sussex

and Kent. . . . The Group catered predominantly to the
metropolitan middle-class audience . . .

(John Elsom, *Post-War British Theatre*, Routledge & Kegan
Paul, 1979, pp. 18, 36)

But Elsom also notes in passing the way that changes in the
family life of this audience were lightly reflected in the plays
themselves:

> Many comedies after the war had shown middle-class
> families in difficulties, either financial ones . . . marital ones
> or generation squabbles. . . . These problems, however, could
> be solved (and usually were) and they did not challenge the
> basis of middle-class life. The comedies of middle-class
> decline were not radical in the sense that they attacked the
> bourgeoisie from the standpoint (say) of a Brechtian Marxist,
> but they did present a picture of seedy snobbery, of sexual
> hypocrisy and of social failure unredeemed by idealism.
>
> (*Ibid.*, p. 93)

Commercial, West End theatre was only able to pay lip-service
to these new social pressures; the real impact and changes within
theatre work were happening elsewhere. Community-based plays
(particularly those done by Joan Littlewood at the Theatre Royal
in Stratford, East London in the 1950s, and by Peter Cheeseman
at Stoke-on-Trent in the 1960s) turned their attention to the lives
of ordinary people as the subject matter for drama (as in Stoke's
special brand of documentary theatre about local people and their
history and lives) and in popular entertainment forms enjoyed by
working-class people (as at the Theatre Royal). At the avant-garde
end of theatre work the influences of Stanislavsky and the American
Method school of acting produced experiments with ensemble
work and encouraged the establishment of permanent theatre
companies (in the work of directors like George Devine and Michel
Saint-Denis). Greater interest in the work of European dramatists
throughout the 1950s (including Brecht) opened a fruitful channel
for exploring new forms and approaches. The mixture of working-
class realism, absurdism and didacticism which fed into the revival
of agitprop from 1968 onwards thus has its aesthetic and social
foundations in the 1950s. In addition, the objective changes taking

place in the family and the position of women introduced a new aspect to the post-1968 protest.

The Women's Liberation Movement and feminism

The 'permissive society' of the late 1960s claimed to be flinging aside the last vestiges of Victorian morality; the student movement of 1968 claimed to be politicising daily life. As some women tried to act out the counter-cultural liberation for themselves, they discovered that the double standard which made Victorian morality so hypocritical was still in operation:

> Glance at any left theoretical journal or go to any large meeting, you won't find many articles either by or about women and you won't see many women speaking. Think of the way women relate to the left groups. Very largely we complement the men: we hold small groups together, we send out reminders, we type the leaflets, we administer rather than initiate. . . . Revolutionary students are quite capable of wolf-whistling and cat-calling when a girl speaks; more common though is tolerant humour, patronising derision or that silence after which everyone continues as if nobody had spoken.
>
> (Sheila Rowbotham, 'Women's Liberation and the New Politics', in *The Body Politic*, compiled by M. Wandor, Stage 1, 1972, p. 22)

The relatively privileged, highly articulate world of student protest was still male-dominated. The formation of the Women's Liberation Movement in Britain, which held its first national conference in the spring of 1970, came from three immediate sources: from within the student movement; from attention drawn to the position of working-class women through a series of industrial disputes during 1968; and from middle-class women able to express the discontents prompted by the frustration of unrelenting housewifery.

The conference was held at Ruskin College in Oxford; originally conceived as a weekend history workshop organised by women at the college, it soon took on a more immediate and urgent impetus.

Over 500 women came from all over the country, and by the end of the weekend four basic 'demands' had been formulated: (1) Equal Pay. (2) Equal Education and Opportunity. (3) 24–Hour Nurseries. (4) Free Contraception and Abortion on Demand. The demands were a simple expression of desires for material change to improve the position of women. The demands also made a clear link between women's relationship to (a) material social production; (b) the family; (c) individual sexual choice. This new wave of feminism aimed to embrace all areas of experience, and to draw attention in a new way to the relationship between the social and sexual division of labour.

Sexism was coined by analogy with the term *racism* in the American civil rights movement in the early 1960s. Defined simply, sexism refers to the systematic ways in which men and women are brought up to view each other antagonistically, on the assumption that the male is always superior to the female. It is consequently necessary for women themselves to internalise this ideology and believe themselves inferior if they are to accept their given role. The struggle for feminists was therefore not only to challenge male power, but to encourage women to counteract their own passivity; to resist the assumption that women are only important in terms of their relationships with men, or as secondary citizens. Such assumptions divide women from each other, and make them compete with each other for male attention. The very day-to-day currency of ordinary conversation assumes that the male pronoun 'he' will stand for the universal experience, and that the subject matter for culture and art is always seen from the point of view of the male protagonist(s).

Feminism, then, challenges a number of assumptions about women and men: (a) that men are the centre of the universe; (b) that women are secondary and dependent on men; (c) that the social/sexual division of labour is 'natural' and unchanging.

At the beginning of the 1970s the Women's Liberation Movement set great store by the process of *consciousness-raising*, where small groups of women met, and in an informal atmosphere discovered and began to understand the nature of an oppression which permeates the most private emotions as well as the more easily identifiable political arenas such as equal pay. In such groups women developed solidarity and 'sisterhood', free of the inhibiting presence of men. The 'separatism' of such groups (or indeed any groups in which women meet without men) has always aroused great controversy, but it has been a vital element in the process of changing the situation of women. Because many women absorb a view of themselves as inferior (even though objective reality often contradicts that feeling), organising separately enables women to discover their strengths, with each other's support. For many women, too, the discovery that friendship with women (sexual or not) can be fulfilling has also been important in developing both individual and political self-determination. The slogan that 'the personal is political' was taken up by feminists to mean that there is no aspect of 'personal' experience which cannot be analysed and understood and changed – albeit slowly and painfully. It was also taken up as a corrective to the classical socialist assumption that the liberation of women would follow the economic revolution (i.e., the transferring of ownership of the means of production from individuals to the people).

During 1970–2 the media took up 'Women's Lib' (as they termed it with an abbreviated sneer) and ridiculed it. But the Movement continued to grow. After a march through London to celebrate International Women's Day in 1971 the number of groups in London grew to over one hundred. By 1972 the Women's Liberation Movement was beginning to establish its own communications network. That year four journals started: the monthly *Spare Rib*, launched by women who had mainly worked for the 'underground' press and who wanted to put their skills to use in a cause with which they could identify; the bi-monthly *Women's Report* which collated news and comment about women; *Women's Voice*, produced by women in the International Socialist group; and *Red Rag*, put out by an editorial collective of women within the Communist Party and unaligned socialist-feminists.

The latter gave expression to a further development in British feminism, involving a new approach to the basis of class analysis. The roots of the new feminist theory had come from America – where radical movements did not develop in the context of an organised labour movement, and where Marxism has therefore had less impact on political theory. American 'radical feminism' followed on from Betty Friedan's *The Feminine Mystique* in emphasising those qualities which unite women across classes, on the basis of their biological and social functions in the family. This is, of course, something of a simplification – but the basic distinction between *radical* and *socialist* feminism is that the former assumes that sexism is the root of all other antagonisms in society, and envisages some kind of revolution of women (the oppressed) against the oppressors (men, or the patriarchy) to change things. Socialist feminism attempts to relate a class analysis to an analysis of sexism, and to decide on the best organisational and strategic way to change both economic exploitation based on class and oppression based on gender. But both strands of feminism agree on the need to challenge male dominance and female passivity wherever it is found. (See Chapters 8 and 11 for a more updated and elaborated discussion of the various feminist tendencies in relation to the work of women playwrights.)

During 1973–4 a series of socialist-feminist conferences was held in different parts of the country. In 1974 an initiative came from men and women in the labour movement: a Working Women's Charter was drawn up, elaborating the original four Ruskin demands into a longer programme of ten. In 1975 the Trades Union Congress revived their charter for Women at Work, and the two documents provided a possible programme for feminists to improve the position of women within the trade union movement.

During the 1970s both formal and informal attempts were made to redress the imbalance of power between the sexes, and indeed to politicise the issue of sexual choice itself. The Women's Liberation Movement laid great stress on anti-authoritarian ways of working; it also drew in women from different class backgrounds and with different feminist allegiances. It did not develop either a national organisation or political structures which could plan and implement either a broad radical– or socialist-feminist strategy. The consequences for this have been both positive and negative. It has meant that feminism sometimes appears diffuse and difficult to define, and is not always as politically effective as it might be. But the very lack of rigid organisation has also enabled a plurality of issues to be challenged; it also reflects the objective problem of linking campaigns for legislative change (such as the campaign for equal pay), which are about external conditions of work, with the more subtle implications of changing people's attitudes to each other and to their own self-image. In particular the question of

organisation highlights the difficulties facing feminists who challenge inequalities within the home, in the family, in attitudes to
housework and sexuality, where the struggle still takes place behind
closed doors, in 'private'. One could say that in the second half of
the 1970s, as the Women's Liberation Movement receded as an
identifiable entity, feminism gained in confidence and diversity.

In the first half of the 1980s the contours of feminism have
changed yet again. On the one hand certain influences are very
clearly evident: in the success of publishing ventures such as Virago
and the Women's Press, and in the active presence of many feminists in local government and in parts of the trade union movement.
The currency of certain basic ideas associated with feminism is
more common; it is no longer considered explosive to suggest that
in education, for example, there is still a long way to go before
the distinction between girls' and boys' subjects can be abolished,
or to claim that in many jobs women still have fewer prospects
than men. The very word 'feminist' itself is no longer seen as the
corrosive term of abuse which it was at the beginning of the 1970s.
But it would be naive to claim that everything has changed for
women. The first half of the 1980s has seen the rapid rise of
unemployment levels unheard of since the 1930s, and a very
contradictory situation in which feminist consciousness in some
quarters has been heightened throughout the 1970s, without many
of the material conditions to make improvements for women possible. There are also new generations of young men and women
who often assume that the need for feminism is over, that all the
sound and fury was necessary in the 1970s, but is no longer. The
phenomena of androgynous fashion, of gender-bending in the pop
world, of certain manifestations of fashionable homosexuality and
bi-sexuality, sometimes give the impression that we are living in a
metropolitan post-feminist world. The reality is that some aspects
of feminism have been effective, some have become more sophisticated, but political and personal life are full of areas where the
position of women has remained unchanged, and where the work
of feminist critiques and action are still as necessary as they ever
were.

The Gay Liberation Front and gay politics

When a law was passed against homosexuality in 1885, it was only male homosexuality which was made criminal. Because male friendship and association is more visible in all classes, late-Victorian moral stringency assumed that women did not associate with each other, but rather related to society only via men. Thus male homosexuality could be acknowledged while female homosexuality was denied; male homosexuality threatened the image of the virile heterosexual male – and by extension threatened the very backbone of the family.

The constitutional attempt to repress homosexuality helped spur the campaigns of social and political radicals:

> from the 1880s to the 1920s the most sympathetic supporters
> for sex reform in general and homosexual reform in
> particular had come from the left; and, as a corollary, most
> of the reformers were clearly men and women of the left.
> But the theoretical and practical problems that this
> connection raised had never been clearly explored. . . . One
> of the problems was that there was no fully worked-out
> theoretical position on women and sexuality in the socialist
> tradition.
>
> (Jeff Weeks, *Coming Out*, Quartet, 1977, p. 144)

During the 1920s and 1930s feminist and sexual reform campaigns in Britain lost impetus; in addition, the Soviet ideology of the 1930s produced a backlash against homosexuality, which was seen at best as an example of bourgeois decadence, and at worst, as a symptom of fascism. It was not until the 1950s and 1960s, in a climate of change in the organisation of family life and the liberalisation of laws on sexuality, that campaigns were renewed, resulting in the partial decriminalisation of male homosexuality in 1967.

In the autumn of 1970 the Gay Liberation Front (GLF) formed in Britain – like the Women's Liberation Movement, on the wave of radical movements developing out of 1968. The term 'gay' meant prostitute in the nineteenth century and, before it was adopted by the Gay Liberation Front, was mainly used as a term for upper-class, homosexual meeting places. Like the Women's

Liberation Movement, the Gay Liberation Front's articulate minority was largely middle class; in its early stages it was also predominantly male. Because male homosexuality had only recently been decriminalised, much of the Gay Liberation Front's concern was to encourage open and proud demonstration of male homosexual relationships, in reaction against the shadowy ghetto-like culture of their pre-1967 lifestyle:

> In the GLF this change revolved around three basic concepts: first, the idea of 'coming out', of being open about one's homosexuality, of rejecting the shame and guilt and the enforced 'double life', of asserting 'gay pride' and 'gay anger' around the cry 'out of the closets, into the streets'. Secondly, the idea of 'coming together', of solidarity and strength coming through collective endeavour, and of the mass confrontation of oppression. And thirdly, and centrally, the identification of the roots of oppression in the concept of sexism and of exploring the means to extirpate it.
>
> (Weeks, *ibid.*, p. 191)

The connections between the roots of gay oppression and the oppression of women were clearly made; but at the same time different forms of gay oppression were identified, and although the Gay Liberation Front continued meeting formally until 1972, these differences helped lead to its dispersion. In particular, the conflict between gay men and lesbians proved problematic; women were a minority in the Gay Liberation Front, and they felt that general patterns of male dominance in society were being reproduced within a supposedly radical movement. Even though lesbians and gay men shared a sense of hostility from the dominant heterosexual society, lesbians felt they also had to deal with prejudice against them as women, both from 'straight' society and from many gay men.

After 1972 gay activism continued (*Gay News* began publication that year and continued until 1983), but generally in separate male and female groupings. Living openly as homosexuals remained crucially important for all gays, and whereas for many this consti-tuted the sum of their politics, others saw the oppression of gays also in terms of gender and class conflict. In lifestyle and sexual choice gay politics made a particular contribution to the way feminism linked sexual oppression with the family. Although their claims were perhaps oversimplified, they were able to pinpoint accurately the 'threat' they were seen as posing:

> in some ways [we] are already more advanced than straight people. We are already outside the family, and we have already, in part, at least, rejected the 'masculine' and 'feminine' roles society has designed for us. . . . Gay men don't need to oppress women in order to fulfil their own psycho-sexual needs, and gay women don't have to relate sexually to the male oppressor, so that at this moment in time the freest and most equal relationships are likely to be between homosexuals.
>
> (GLF Manifesto, 1970)

And gay men were also the first men to discuss openly the repressiveness of their own masculine conditioning.

2

Cross-dressing, sexual representation and the sexual division of labour in theatre

This book focuses on sexual representation in two senses: firstly in the way that women are represented in the theatre (both as workers and as they are presented and represented onstage, in the form and content of plays); and secondly in the way in which homosexuals (male and female) and homosexuality (male and female) appear in theatre. Although they sometimes tend to be seen as separate issues, there are in fact interesting historical and stylistic connections between the two aspects. There is the obvious point that both kinds of representation suffer from a history of taboos of different kinds: in many Western countries women were forbidden to act on the 'respectable' stage until a mere 400 years ago. Gay men and women have always worked in theatre (as in other industries) but the taboos against the public recognition of homosexuality has meant that their relationship to their work has always had something of a covert nature.

Different theatrical conventions have contained within them the signs of these constraints and taboos, often to the point of a new kind of erotic stimulus. Before women officially appeared onstage as actresses in the seventeenth century (travelling groups of players, who did not perform in theatre buildings, often included women), the accepted practice was that boys or young men played the parts of the female characters. This is received wisdom about the practice in Shakespeare's day, and it is easy to imagine that it was just taken for granted. In fact this purely functional use of 'cross-dressing' caused a great deal of moral concern, as Lisa Jardine points out:

the taking of female parts by boy players actually occasioned a good deal of contemporary comment, and created considerable moral uneasiness, even amongst those who patronised and supported the theatres.

(*Still Harping on Daughters*, Harvester Press, 1983, p. 9)

One of the reasons why the theatre was seen as encouraging immorality was connected with the complex erotic response of the audience to the performance of boys in the female roles. Recalling the prohibition in Deuteronomy – 'The woman shall not wear that which pertaineth unto a man, neither shall a man put on a woman's garment: for all that do so are abomination unto the Lord their God' (22:5), some Elizabethans saw the stage presentation of boys wearing women's clothes as letting loose a whole nest of sexual vipers:

Sexuality, misdirected towards the boy masquerading in female dress, is 'stirred' by attire and gesture; male prostitution and perverted sexual activity is the inevitable accompaniment of female impersonation.

(Jardine, *ibid.*, p. 9)

And the erotic implications become even more complex when it is a boy, masquerading as a woman dressed as a boy. The puns about cross-dressing which Shakespeare used, the use of dramatic irony (the audience knows that there is a double level of deception – the cross-dressed 'character' and the cross-dressed boy performer), produced an erotic charge which depended on the combination of associations with sexual attraction towards boys and women:

the dependent role of the boy player doubles for the dependency which is woman's lot, creating a sensuality which is independent of the desired figure, and which is particularly erotic where the sex is confused (when boy player represents woman, disguised as dependent boy).

(Jardine, *ibid.*, p. 24)

These complex erotic implications might have had (probably still have today) different impacts on the men and women in the audience. For men, perhaps, there was the permanent suggestion of subtextual homo-eroticism; for women, perhaps, a kind of displaced narcissism, in which they could see their sex 'played' by a young boy, who could simultaneously represent innocence and potential virility. One can only imagine what an Elizabethan audience might have absorbed emotionally, but given the very complex way in which the sexual/erotic works in art, it is fascinating to see the different functions which cross-dressing has had in the past, and the implications which it can have in the present.

Male cross-dressing in the Elizabethan era came about as a consequence of society's taboos on women in the theatre. Officially, women were not allowed to perform in 'serious' drama in England, as a result of the Christian Church's response to the theatre. In her book *Enter the Actress* Rosamond Gilder explains the way in which the Church's attitude to the theatre itself, and to the role of women as public performers were interwoven:

> The war between Church and stage has been long and bitter,
> particularly in the early days when the theatre represented
> the last entrenched camp of paganism, and as such was the
> subject of virulent attack and condemnation. The Church
> desired nothing less than the complete annihilation of its
> enemy, and in this, by the close of the fourth century, it
> had largely succeeded.
>
>   (*Enter the Actress*, Theatre Arts Books, 1931, p. 18)

With an effective ban on theatre per se, the question of whether or not women could perform was entirely hypothetical. But the Church had its own forms of theatrical ritual in public religious services, and here the attitudes to women participating in any form of public ceremonial or performance were clear:

> Women were not allowed to speak in church even for the
> praiseworthy purposes of exhortation and prayer; how
> much less would they be tolerated as performers in its sacred
> mysteries. In a woodcut dating from the twelfth century a
> group of women are shown suffering extreme torment in a
> flamy hell for the nefarious sin of having raised their voices
> in church. Silenced and forced to cover their heads for greater
> modesty, excluded from the performance of any sacred
> office, and relegated to a properly subordinate position, there
> was no possibility of women taking part in religious plays,

except when they were performed in the seclusion of their own world of the convents.

(Ibid., p. 46)

For men it was thus still possible to perform in public, to give voice, either through religious service or through religious drama; but for women both were very clearly taboo. In other parts of Europe things were less stringent – women were part of the commedia dell'arte groups in Italy, and performed in travelling shows – though a sixteenth-century Papal edict banned them from appearing on 'serious' stages. The very idea that a woman might play any part other than that assigned to her, coupled with the dangers of erotic excitement in the spectators, combined to suggest that actresses and prostitution were merely synonyms. As we have seen from the anxiety about boy players impersonating women, quoted earlier, simply excluding women from the stage did not allay fears about sexual titillation, but the prevailing nervousness about what would happen if women were let loose onstage meant that when royal patents were granted to two theatres in 1660, cautionary words about decency and women were included:

> And forasmuch as many plays formerly acted do contain several profane, obscene, and scurrilous passages, and the women's parts therein have been acted by men in the habits of women, at which some have taken offence; for the preventing of these abuses for the future we do strictly charge, command and enjoin that from henceforth no new play shall be acted by either of the said companies containing any passage offensive to piety and good manner. . . . And we do likewise permit and give leave that all the women's parts to be acted in either of the said two companies from this time to come may be performed by women, so long as these recreations, which by reason of the abuses aforesaid were scandalous and offensive, may by such reformation be esteemed not only harmless delights, but useful and instructive representations of human life, by such of our good subjects as shall resort to see the same.

So while 'admitting' women to the stage was an important professional step forward, the ostensible aim of such an action was to lend the right kind of moral tone to the theatre. From being seen as little short of a whore, the actress was now seen as the potential shining light of decency. But with actresses now part of the official theatre world, very soon they became the source of a different kind of cross-dressing – women in men's clothes, in the 'breeches parts', which displayed women's legs, and which were the precursor of the convention of the pantomime principal boy played by a woman. Yet again anxiety about the immorality of the theatre and the dangers of the appeal of female sexuality found public voice in the words of John Evelyn in 1666:

> This night . . . was acted by Lord Broghill's tragedy call'd
> *Mustapha* before their Majesties at Court, at which I was
> present, very seldom going to the public theatres for many
> reasons, now as they are abused to an atheistical liberty,
> fowle and undecent women now . . . permitted to appear and
> to act, who inflaming several young noblemen and gallants,
> became their misses, and to some their wives . . . to the
> reproach of their noble families and ruine of both body and
> soule.
>
> (Quoted in *Enter the Actress*, pp. 170–1)

The appeal and fashion of cross-dressing for women and men has continued in various forms. For actresses it has meant an extension of emotional possibility – an actress playing the character of Hamlet, as so many have, covers a far greater emotional range than she would if she were playing Ophelia. In some way too the complexities of erotic appeal apply to the way an audience sees a woman playing 'male' emotions, 'male' actions, which will have their own reverberations. In the nineteenth century the music hall created the individual performance art of male and female impersonation, and Vesta Tilley, the most successful of these, was aware that the sexuality conveyed by her personality was tinged with ambiguity:

> It may be because I generally appeared on stage as a young
> man that a big percentage of my admirers were women.
> Girls of all ages would wait in crowds to see me enter or
> leave the theatre, and each post brought me piles of letters
> varying from impassioned declarations of undying love to a

request for an autograph, or photograph, or a simple
flower, or a piece of ribbon I had worn.
(Quoted in *Innocent Flowers*, Julie Holledge, Virago, 1981,
p. 21)

Vesta Tilley's own attitude appears to be ambiguous as regards
the kinds of fantasy she may have aroused in her women fans.
What is interesting about all forms of cross-dressing, whether in
'serious' or 'popular' art forms, is that they have the potential to
arouse erotic responses in both men and women. Obviously the
theatrical and social conventions of different periods will dictate
the different ways in which cross-dressing is either functional, or
a symptom of creative responses suppressed in other areas, or
forms of freedom of expression for performers. It is also interesting
to note that cross-dressing, or transvestite theatre, has flourished
during historical periods when attitudes to sexuality and the
position of women have been challenged – during the Restoration,
through the nineteenth century when the industrial revolution
altered the face of urban and family life, and in certain respects in
today's theatre. At such times of social questioning and change,
there is clearly a tension between the dominant expectations of
how men and women are supposed to feel and behave – i.e., what
is considered properly 'masculine' or 'feminine', and the changing
reality of people's lives. Cross-dressing in whatever theatrical form
can serve both as symptom and response to this tension. It can
function as an indirect effort to contain rebellion – i.e., any departure from the accepted 'norms' of masculine and feminine – by
ridiculing any departure from the status quo; we can see some of
the legacy of that in certain pantomime dame caricatures, who
produce a stream of misogynist jokes. But it can also function as
an expression of rebellion; a form of witty subversion in which
one sex impersonates the other, and by so doing shows up some of
the ridiculous constraints which define femininity and masculinity.
Not surprisingly many of the theatrical traditions which make
use of cross-dressing have also been associated with gay subculture,
since men and women whose emotional and sexual lives are
engaged with members of their own sex challenge in a very fundamental way the dominant assumptions that all people 'are' hetero-

sexual and are expected to conform to the norms of conventional familial lifestyles.

Having said that, however, it is clear that even here there is a gender imbalance. While the theatrical traditions of 'camp' and 'drag' have their roots in the relationship of women to the theatre, as well as to the relationship of homosexuals to the theatre, their history has been largely dominated by men, for the same reasons that other theatre forms have been male-dominated.

> There was no visible subculture for lesbians until later in this century, unlike the situation for male homosexuals. And lesbianism was not illegal so there were few spectacular court cases and no compelling reason for a political campaign on the question.
>
> (Jeff Weeks, *Coming Out*, Quartet, 1977, pp. 65–6)

The male gay subculture, until the change in the law in 1967, existed as a space within which men could express and explore a tabooed sexuality. And within the artistic professions it was possible for many male homosexuals to find a paradoxical place – known within the professions to be homosexual, but screened from being publicly exposed as such. One can see why this was professionally possible – particularly in the visual, domestic and theatrical arts – because of the way in which the characteristics demanded for those professions are seen as a mixture of the 'conventionally' masculine and the 'conventionally' feminine – as long, that is, as those with a mixture of the required characteristics are male. Sensitivity and emotional expression (the feminine) can be combined with ambition and ruthlessness (the masculine) – in men:

> The artistic sphere has long been claimed by gay men as legitimate territory: in this area the male homosexual has found the means to pass by identifying himself as artistic/romantic rather than simply gay. So the social rejection on the basis of sexuality is refocused by the justification of art.
>
> (Caroline Sheldon, *Gays and Film*, British Film Institute, 1977, p. 10)

Since all homosexuals had to 'put on an act' in order to survive in society as individuals, the dividing line between life and art is thus blurred:

> The art of passing [for straight] is an acting part; to pass is to be 'on stage', to impersonate heterosexual citizenry, to pretend to be a real (i.e., straight) man or woman.
>
> (Jack Babuscio, *Gays and Film*, p. 45)

The higher profile of the 'camp' and 'high camp' in the 1950s and 1960s exercised the attention of many cultural critics, and its complex ambiguity was wrestled with in an aphoristic essay by Susan Sontag in 1964:

> one way of seeing the world as an aesthetic phenomenon . . . in terms of artifice or stylisation. . . . To emphasise style is to slight content, or to introduce an attitude which is neutral with respect to content.
>
> (*Notes Against Interpretation*, Dell, 1969, p. 279)

Thus the male homosexual tradition, while highly self-conscious, and always in some sense aware of its relationship to dominant representations of maleness and femaleness, has not hitherto defined itself as 'political'. It has largely been a comment from within theatre on its own artifice, celebrating the illusion of theatrical performance in its own way. Of course there have occasionally been subversive elements, but there have also often been moments when camp and drag have been defensive, expressing themselves only through the art, within the confined freedom of the stage performance, and leaving life precisely where it is, unchallenged. The oppressions and hostilities which gay people experienced were thus transposed from social problem into the solution of theatrical style. Performance was perceived to be the answer, rather than a change in social reality – a pre-political cultural expression for the gay perception and imagination. It can be seen, then, that while male homosexuals would always have felt themselves in an ambiguous position, they still would not have felt as powerful a taboo as either lesbians or women in certain areas of theatre work. Male homosexuals had exciting theatrical styles, a certain camaraderie, and in certain kinds of area of authority – as directors, and in specific performance areas such as dance

– a very positive chance to express those areas of their creativity normally divided into the 'masculine' and the 'feminine'.

For women the situation has been rather different. There has been no thorough, across the board survey done of where women work in the theatre industry, but it is still possible to analyse the male-female ratio in the workforce, by taking into account the assumptions which underlie the way the industry is structured – in terms of both the social and the sexual divisions of labour – i.e., where people work according to a conventional hierarchy of power, and where people work according to assumptions about sexual and gender power.

Traditionally the theatre gives more credit and status to the 'creative' and artistic jobs than it does to the merely functional or technical. So the histories of important theatres or companies are seen to be to the credit of the artistic directors; playwrights (paradoxically, as we shall see later) are seen as the emblems of any period of theatre history – in part the ironic consequence of the fact that some play texts are published and therefore are available to future historians, whereas the work of the director, performer, etc., is rarely if ever on record, and is remembered through anecdote and other kinds of fragmented record. The consequence for writers is ironic, since the theatre history of the past 300 years has been in the control of directors, or actor (sic)-managers, or theatre owners. There is nothing inherently wrong with the fact that the history of theatre is mostly seen as the history of its great plays, if one understands theatre history. Given that the literary traditions of play-writing are also connected with other literary forms, such as the novel and poetry, there will always be particular attention paid to plays as written texts, as well as texts which are blueprints for performance. Because this textual attention is sometimes one-sided, it is very important indeed to remind people that writing for the theatre consists of not only the writer's skill, but the consciousness that the next stage for the text involves the collaboration of all kinds of other theatrical skills. It is of course a truism that in the majority of theatres the writer initiates the text and the director initiates its interpretation; but neither could function were it not for other skills, and when writing and directing are crudely categorised as 'creative', then the initiatives of, say, lighting or set construction are rarely recognised to the same degree.

This hierarchy of status has further implications for the gender divide. It is interesting to note that men dominate at both ends of this status scale: in the artistically authoritative voices of writer and director, and in the technological and manual areas of backstage production. Here again it is useful to make comparisons between the theatre and other industries – cultural and non-cultural. Across the board in the cultural industries men far outnumber women in positions of power; artistic status and artistic power are dominated by men. Similarly, in non-cultural industries, manual labour and most branches of technology are also dominated by men. When these skills are brought to bear on the production of plays, the same pattern of employment prevails. It is also significant that both 'ends' of the status scale, as I have described them, are relatively highly paid.

In the middle strata of the theatrical employment field the divisions between men and women are rather more blurred: for example, women have traditionally (since the nineteenth century) worked as designers, although almost all the 'top' theatre designers are male. In the theatre women tend to work in areas which reflect their 'servicing' roles in other industries and in the domestic division of labour: in middle management, in jobs to do with personnel, casting, or wardrobe – jobs in which looking after people (often with some power, it must be acknowledged) is paramount.

Women are significantly numerous in two areas: the traditional female jobs of secretarial and administration, and theatre publicity; and, of course, where they are irreplaceable because of the gender demands of the job – as actresses.

Women are thus very unevenly distributed throughout the profession, rarely reaching higher than middle management, and, with the notable recent exception of Joan Littlewood and one or two others, rarely functioning, and then not for long, as artistic directors of theatres. This is in marked contrast to the amateur theatre field, which, since its rapid expansion in the 1920s and 1930s, is dominated by women. While women have figured prominently in the development of the novel, they have figured only sporadically in the visible history of play-writing. Most permanent theatre companies consist of more men than women (in keeping with the casting demands of both the classical canon and the contemporary repertory theatre fare), and in a profession dogged by high unemployment the average earnings of actresses are lower than those of actors (stars are always the exceptions). On the technical side, women remain in the minority, a combination of prejudice against them, and a hesitancy on the part of women themselves. The 'servicing' areas in which women dominate bear an interesting relationship to both the functions of publicity and actress – indicating that attitudes to women in the various theatre skills are closely related to the function of women in the sexual imagery of our culture.

This sexual imagery is seen at its most explicit, and at its most attractive, often, in advertising imagery, both televisual and magazine. Here various ranges of acceptable (even occasionally dangerous) heterosexuality are used for commercial ends. In the past fifteen years there have been many radical critiques of the ways in which advertising is constructed, what the images mean, how they work on the consumer (whether s/he buys the product is in one sense irrelevant, since these are images which are consumed for pleasure as well as use). And even though fashion and the turnover of current ideas always ensures that images are constantly renewed, very little has fundamentally changed in the past fifteen years. The image of women conveyed by such advertising is divided into two categories: the pre-marital, sexily available female, or the various versions of the post-sexual wife and mother. The two images represent a kind of 'story'; the wild, glamorous woman becomes tamed for the family ads, and her sexuality, at first a challenge, is subsequently contained and virtually disappears. Of course there are stereotyped images of men too, but they cover a far wider range, and there is a sense in which at whatever stage of life a man is represented, he will carry overtones of power and sexual potential. The images of women function as fantasy models for the women viewers, and as potential and desirable objects for the men viewers; in a very crucial sense women are at the centre of the very idea of glamour; but in an ironic fashion, they are also crucial behind the scenes, not just as models, but as servicers of the entertainment and advertising industries themselves. It is as if these women were somehow selling an image of themselves to themselves, in the interest of perpetuating a status quo in which they are ultimately secondary and less powerful than their male 'owners' or 'possessors'. This doesn't mean that there are not powerful spin-offs for the women – modelling, stardom, money, comfort, security – but it highlights the way in which the private role of all women is pointed and reinforced in the shop window of advertising's fantasy imagery. Woman as sexual object must be tamed because female sexuality is seen as something dangerous and uncontainable.

Such assumptions – not always consciously perceived – inevitably spill over into the way the actress/model's offstage persona is presented by the media. Ideally, the more glamorously she can be represented in real life – the more her 'stage' roles (advertising or showbiz/theatre) fit perfectly with her personal life-roles – the simpler and more saleable is her total self as commodity. The concern which television soap operas have for the private morals of their stars indicates that this desire to make public image and private reality conform is still around. And this consumerist need to keep the role image clear explains why it is that the glamour and sales functions are merged in the publicity departments of the theatre, and why these jobs are so often performed by women. The theatre publicity officer is at the sales counter – selling the play to the press, the critics, the rest of the industry, and thus to the public. She tends to present a low-key glamour image in order to sugar the commercial sell, leaving the actress to have the more high-key glamour image. Doing publicity is, of course, a skilled job in its own right, and these comments do not devalue that skill; they are merely intended to show that the significance of the way female sexuality functions and is used affects the industrial process in theatre. Women and men do not have the work roles they do out of sheer accident, and although the theatre is a relatively poor relation in terms of glamour, compared to Hollywood, for example, the same principles still apply.

It is not, therefore, surprising, given the ambiguous relationship between women and the theatre, that women should have been secondarily reflected in the subject matter of plays. The majority of plays for the professional theatre have been written from a male perspective, expressing dramatic action, conflict and development within systems of ideas in which the male concern is the norm. This is not to say that these plays can be crudely categorised and dismissed as 'male', or that they are of no interest to women. The contrary: to see that the dramatic visions of our past have been shaped as much by the genders of their creators as by all the other possible socially determining factors is to gain additional insight into the nature of theatre. The female characters in such plays – even when they appear to be 'heroines' – fit into the spectrum of male-gendered concerns, but rarely shifting the territory explored to that of female experience or female perspective. Women characters thus have been either adjuncts to the main action (often absolutely vital adjuncts, but nevertheless secondary) or have acted as ciphers, objects of displacement for the male protagonists. It has only been when women writers appear in any force that the male-centredness of this territory has been challenged. And until very recently, this has applied as much to political, or socialist theatre, as to the 'establishment' variety.

It was in the context of this male-centred, and heterosexual-dominated perspective that the post-1968 theatre revolution happened. The received state of theatre was one which represented women unevenly as workers throughout the industry, and either partially or distortedly in the matter of plays themselves. Gay men have had certain limited forms of acceptance, but have still benefited from the custom of male-dominance, and have still been more likely to gain positions of prestige and artistic freedom than all women. The 1970s introduced a new political consciousness to the experience of being female and being gay, and it is alongside this new and developing consciousness that the alternative theatre was infused with many and varied sexual-political concerns and interests.

Alternative theatre and sexual politics

Feminist and gay theatre work in the 1970s and 1980s falls into four phases. Phase one covers 1969–73, during the diverse activism (political and cultural) which followed the 1968 events, during the formation of the Women's Liberation Movement and the Gay Liberation Front, and in the context of industrial militancy in Britain which followed the anti-working-class measures introduced by the Conservative government of 1970–4. The alternative theatre movement during this period included a tremendously varied spread of events: arts lab 'happenings', the growth of lunchtime theatre, avant-garde and experimental writing, and self-consciously socialist companies whose work was largely built around responses to different 'issues' – such as tenants organising against rent increases. These plays were mobile, taking theatre to the 'people'; agitprop in both style and intention. The ideology was largely collectivist and libertarian. A strong emphasis on street theatre, taking its content from the early feminist analysis of passive femininity and women's place in the family. Vivid and larger-than-life imagery, the language as simple as possible. This was followed by a kind of indoor agitprop, theatre in buildings (though not always theatre buildings), which followed the format of the male-dominated agitprop: naturalistic 'telling-it-like-it-is' scenes, punctuated by music, rock or pastiche pop, cartoon-like characters. Theatre used very much as a consciousness-raiser, with performance followed by discussion. Very much of its time in rejecting the function of writer and director as part of the oppressive apparatus of conventional theatre.

Phase two covers 1973–7, a period during which working-class militancy abated (after the return of a Labour government in 1974), and during which the expansion of alternative theatre was given a more solid underpinning via state subsidy. Arts Council subsidy to new writing, touring groups and 'fringe' theatres increased dramatically between 1971 and 1978. Linked with this was the spread of trade union militancy among theatre workers (particularly in the performers' union, Equity), and the efforts of alternative theatre itself to begin organising. In 1972 an Association of Lunchtime Theatres was formed, 'to promote lunchtime theatre, to present principally new and neglected plays and playwrights, to provide alternative venues for actors, directors and designers, to encourage audiences by making them more accessible'. In 1974 The Association of Community Theatre (TACT) held its first conference; one of its aims was to put pressure on the Arts Council for subsidy which would enable them to pay Equity minimum wages. Shortly afterwards the Independent Theatres Council drew in individuals and theatres not already covered by TACT, and the two organisations merged. In October 1975 they held a joint conference at the Oval House in London, to which a number of playwrights were invited. Out of this meeting came the Theatre Writers' Group, which a year later styled itself the Theatre Writers' Union, to campaign for better terms and conditions for writers in the subsidised theatre. Within a couple of years the Theatre Writers' Union was working in co-operation with the Writers' Guild, though the two organisations remained separate. Although debates continue as to whether or not state subsidy is a good thing for an alternative theatre which opposes many of the practices and much of the content of the 'established' theatre, it is undeniable that the presence of subsidy has enabled the alternative theatre to become more professionalised, and in many senses more stable; one of the major lessons of the 1970s concerns the necessity of a militant campaign to retain a stystem of public subsidy to the arts, particularly in the face of the cuts of the early 1980s.

Feminist and gay theatre work consolidated itself in the formation of professional companies – the Women's Theatre Group (1974), Monstrous Regiment (1975–6) and Gay Sweatshop (1976). Feminism was slowly beginning to have an impact on some women working in the professional theatre. The new groups were still working largely collectively, but also with a consciousness towards encouraging work by women and gay writers. In keeping with socialist theatre in general, a tendency to move away from issue-based agitprop, towards a desire for more complexly developed plays, with more concern for the subtleties of character. The play-with-music was still a very strong influence, but the individually written play was beginning to find a voice.

Phase three of feminist and gay theatre work covers from 1977 onwards. The mid-1970s expansion of alternative theatre groups and companies was under attack from 1975, when moves within the Arts Council sought to slow down the flow of subsidy money.

Phase four is represented by the numerous new voices of playwrights, women and male gays, whose work has been written and produced since 1979. Some of these are young writers, writing in a climate of individual confidence which has been produced by the bedrock of work described in the previous phases. Some of the writers have worked their way through and with the various developments in the 1970s to find a stronger, more distinct theatrical confidence and voice. In performance new departures have largely taken the form of a new, 'politicised' cabaret, with performers, male and female, feminist and gay, writing and performing their own material. There has also been some interesting performer response against word-based theatre, and in favour of music, movement and visual imagery.

3
The first phase: 1969–73

Early street theatre

> We're not beautiful, we're not ugly, we're angry.
> (Leaflet, 'Miss World' demonstration, 1970)

The twentieth Miss World contest, organised by Mecca Promotions, took place in the Royal Albert Hall in London, on the evening of 20 November 1970, compered by American comedian Bob Hope. At a pre-arranged signal a group of women interrupted the event, in full view of millions of television viewers. The women threw flour, smoke- and stink-bombs, blew whistles, waved rattles and distributed leaflets to members of the audience, protesting against the objectification of women in beauty contests, which epitomised 'the traditional female road to success'. The women were arrested, Bob Hope cracked a few defensive jokes and the show continued.

The form the interruption took echoed the pattern of many similar events initiated by post-1968 student protest: a spectacular interruption of a public 'spectacle', disrupting an occasion in order to express anger at it and arouse its audience from their passive consumer roles. But the objective and the protesters were different: feminists were registering anger at the commercialising of women's sexuality as it was imagined and packaged for profit by men. Writing about the event later, the protestors described it as:

> a blow against passivity, not only the enforced passivity of

the girls on the stage, but the passivity that we all felt in ourselves.

('Miss World', in *The Body Politic*, compiled by M. Wandor, Stage 1, 1972, p. 252)

The following year, in 1971, there was another demonstration, but this time, because police security was more stringent, the demonstrators paraded round the outside of the Royal Albert Hall. The protest was led by the Women's Street Theatre Group and the all-male Gay Street Theatre Group; they distributed leaflets to make their polemical point against the contest, and the women parodied the contest in *The Flashing Nipple Show*; dressed in dark trousers and tops, each woman had flashing lights fixed at her crotch and on her breasts. Simple satirical imagery heralded the arrival of sexual politics into street theatre, consciously drawing its analysis of the position of women from the Women's Liberation Movement:

> it's in the home, around sexuality, that our oppression bites deepest, holds hardest. The 'left' has always said that the economy, our exploitation, has to be changed first, before our lives, our oppression. We say both have to be changed at once – the struggle against internalised oppression, against how we live our lives, is where we begin, where we've been put. . . . Women's oppression cuts across class, but our roles serve capitalism and are caused and dictated by it.
>
> ('Miss World', p. 260)

The private goes public

Spontaneous and informal feminist and gay street theatre events continued in various parts of the country, but these early years saw a greater expansion of feminist than gay theatre work. It developed from four sources: (1) A further development of feminist agitprop, emerging from the early street theatre. (2) From within the professional theatre. (3) From Theatre-in-Education. (4) From the impact of feminism on socialist companies.

The Women's Street Theatre Group formed during the summer of 1970. Their first main event was at the demonstration to celebrate International Women's Day on 6 March 1971. The group danced along with the marchers, through a spring snow-shower in London, while a record player in a pram played 'Keep Young and Beautiful'. The march ended in Trafalgar Square, and the group performed their first 'play', *Sugar and Spice*, satirising the way women are trapped (a) as sex objects (a continuation of the anti-Miss World theme) and (b) as wives and mothers within the family. A bold imagistic approach featured such intimate objects as a huge deodorant, a large sanitary towel, and a gigantic red, white and blue penis (artificial!). The images were simple and deliberately shocking, breaking taboos about what is considered 'decent' for women to display in public, and challenging the way women's bodies and their sexuality are deliberately hidden and repressed where they don't conform to the dominant sexual imagery. By portraying these 'taboo' objects in a deliberately grotesque and exaggerated way, the audience was challenged to look at its own assumptions about women's sexuality. This approach was also behind the group's subsequent offerings. They staged one event in the ladies' lavatory in the 'Miss Selfridge' shop in Oxford Street, pretending to shave their faces in front of the mirrors in an attempt to get other women to examine their own narcissism in using make-up; another took place on the London underground, where women, dressed as a dolly bird, an academic and a housewife, were auctioned off to the crowd.

In September 1971 the group took part (by invitation) in a demonstration organised by the Christian Festival of Light. There was a placard with 'Holy Family' written on one side (a pun combining Marx's ironic use of the term with the religious concept) and 'Fuck the Family' on the other side, with an asterisk in 'Family', but not in 'Fuck'. There were also two large, white, stuffed hands, one inscribed 'Church', and the other 'State', and chains attaching the hands to a typical hierarchical 'family': the husband beat his wife, the wife beat the child and the child beat up a teddy bear. Accompanying the Women's Street Theatre Group were a number of gay men, dressed as nuns; the tone of the theatrical and satirical imagery led to the women and men being arrested, thereby posing a conundrum for the police: should the men (who 'appeared' to be female) be put with the women, or in a separate cell because they were 'really' men? It was an unintended demonstration of a point that both men and women were trying to make: are gender roles based on biology or social conditioning, on appearance or reality? In the event the men were put in a separate cell.

After the initial spontaneous exhilaration of these street theatre events, the Women's Street Theatre Group began thinking more seriously about their aims and audiences. The Equal Pay Act had been passed in 1970 to a fair amount of fearful feminist publicity about its loopholes, as well as some relief that the principle of equal pay for men and women had been officially recognised. The group began to work on a play about the impact of the Act, intending it as an indoor event, destined for Women's Liberation Movement and trade union audiences. They also changed their name to the more vivid 'Punching Judies', and were now an all-women group (the early street theatre included men). *The Amazing Equal Pay Show* was collectively devised and scripted, in key with the then prevalent practice in political touring groups, in form also following the pattern of early 1970s agitprop: a simple naturalistic story about workers, framed within a pantomime-type cartoon. Capitalist Magician Mr Marvo wore a huge cloak lined with money, and was accompanied by his obedient and sexy sidekick, Poodle; Members of Parliament did deals with each other and with the unions using oversized playing cards. Against this backdrop the women workers began to get together to organise out from the bottom of the capitalist heap, confronting their bosses and their husbands.

The play was based on a strike for equal pay by women machinists at Fords in 1968. Barbara Castle (heavily lampooned throughout) was Minister of Employment in the Labour government at the time. She visited the factory, and eventually helped the women achieve 92 per cent of the money they were demanding. The attitude to class in the play is somewhat ambiguous; the 'divide and rule' approach of capitalism is simply and visually sketched, and the isolation of the women workers against the hostility of their male fellow workers is also demonstrated through the naturalistic 'story'. The exhortatory message behind the play is directed mainly at women in the audience, urging them to see the connections between the struggle at home and the struggle at work. At the same time the play ridicules the men, the trade union bureaucracy and the Labour Party in a way that was theatrically effective but politically naive, since it appeared to attack political organisation as such. However, it was uncompromising in pushing the interests of ordinary women to the fore, showing how deep the division between working-class men and women can be, and pointing out the conflicts between working people's needs at the grassroots, and the demands of Realpolitik at the top. In the process Barbara Castle was portrayed as a woman selling her fellow women out (an oversimplification of her role, since she had helped draw up the Equal Pay Bill):

> Bubble bubble toil and trouble
> In Barbara's cauldron turn to rubble;
> Crouch round while I make my spell
> To give the women workers hell,
> Tongue in cheek and hand on heart
> I'll force the working class apart . . .
> A pinch of promises, gramme of guile
> Well beaten up with serpent's smile;
> Pepper it up with prevarication
> Spice it with negotiation
> Ending differentials makes my tea hot stuff
> So leave it out, there's quite enough
> With higher pay and praise as well
> Their heads will swim, their heads will swell
> So now my tea is strong and sweet
> 'Twill knock those women off their feet.

The play was performed throughout the winter of 1972, and during 1973 a newly formed London Women's Film Group began filming the play, sticking closely to the original script, but filming on location.

The Women's Liberation Movement and professional theatre

In 1969 *Vagina Rex and the Gas Oven* by writer, director and actress Jane Arden was performed at the Drury Lane Arts Lab in London. Professionals Sheila Allen and Victor Spinetti 'starred' in the play, which was a prophetic precursor of some of the feminist concerns in the 1970s. Stylistically it was a montage, exploring a woman's struggle to deal with her sense of her own conditioned inferiority, surreal and mystical by turns, using the mixed-media (strobe lighting, etc.) of the 'acid' 1960s. During the summer of 1970 Jane Arden and Sheila Allen (who was then involved in one of the London consciousness-raising groups) set up meetings to gather a group of women to work on a project of Arden's. A theatre group was formed – defiantly named 'Holocaust' – bringing together women from different artistic backgrounds: a musician, a sculptress, a television director, a professional actress, as well as women who wanted to express their feminism through theatre. The outcome was an extraordinary event performed in 1971: *A New Communion for Freaks, Prophets and Witches* (later made into an equally extraordinary film by Jack Bond called *The Other Side of the Underneath*). The piece was set in a mental hospital, where a group of women are confined because they have been unable to conform to the 'feminine' roles demanded of them by society, and have succumbed to 'madness'. The play was scripted from improvisations, the experiences of the cast, using encounter-group type techniques, in a montage of songs, speeches, dialogue, music and some potent, semi-erotic visual imagery. As against the psychologically destructive effects of conventional 'feminine' conditioning, Arden groped towards exploring some kind of 'female' principle, framed in an abstract cosmic mysticism at the very end of the play, but extraordinarily disturbing and potent in its individual moments – notable among these were a simple 'family doll' song placing the female in a Laingian context of power games, and a half-naked woman with top hat and cane simulating a rape scene with another woman. The theatrical influences came far more from the arts lab mixed-media strand of fringe theatre and from the new Laingian psychology than from street theatre, and translated the let-it-all-hang-out slogans of the hippies into a searing plea to free the crippled creativity of individual women.

Theatre-in-Education and feminism

The Theatre-in-Education (TIE) movement began around 1965, during the expansion of regional work, engaging the energies of radical teachers who were interested in using theatre as a general educational aid in an extension of liberal studies courses. Many students going into Theatre-in-Education from university in the late 1960s and early 1970s took with them a heightened political consciousness and the influence of feminism. So much Theatre-in-Education work is undocumented and ephemeral that it is difficult to know quite how widespread the impact on it of sexual politics was, but one such play has been published, with a lengthy account of its production process. This was *Sweetie Pie*, devised during 1972 by the Bolton Octagon Theatre-in-Education company, taking as its conscious point of departure the four demands formulated at Ruskin, and illustrating their relevance to an ordinary working-class woman.

Drawing on the mixed conventions of the 1970s agitprop, *Sweetie Pie* mixes fantasy with realistic elements: Mr Cash (representing guess what) reads a fairy tale, which is brought to life by Margaret, its central character. It is her 'fairy story' that Mr Cash is telling. She grows up with average female ambitions for a happy marriage-ever-after; then when she has children, she and her husband find they can't manage on his money. She takes a job, is drawn into union activity and has to face her husband's opposition. When she gets pregnant, she also has to face the difficult decision about whether or not to have an abortion. By the end of the play Margaret has become enraged by Mr Cash's fairy-tale ideals about happy wife and motherhood; she flings his story book to the ground, declaring that 'It's all lies'. As well as including in the storyline information about the financial problems faced by women, and about their double role at home and at work, the play also illustrates the way the media tries to contain women's aspirations by beaming out stereotypical images of women. In particular the play pastiches the gormless TV contest, in which participants are reduced to formula responses. *Sweetie Pie* takes the audience through the consciousness-raising process of an individual woman who reaches the point where she refuses to accept the views of the dominant ideology about what she should be; a political parable about an ordinary woman.

Socialist companies and feminism

Red Ladder started in 1968, one of the earliest and longest-lasting of the socialist theatre companies. It was a mixed group, and they planned to do a short play about 'women' as part of a sequence of short 10- to 15-minute 'units' which could be taken out to different audiences. However, by 1972 they had decided that the subject could not be contained in so short a time, and a collectively devised first draft of a longer play was written. This was rejected by the women in the group as being too 'factory-oriented'; the project was left for some months, and then taken up again during 1973. It was first performed under the title of *Strike While the Iron is Hot*[1] in 1974, then retitled *A Woman's Work is Never Done*, and continued in the group's repertoire for over two years.

Like *Sweetie Pie* Red Ladder's play followed the changing experience and consciousness of one working-class woman, from innocent romantic marriage, through children, jobs, trade union consciousness and finally into a new independence both at work and in her relationship with her husband. Helen and Dave's story demonstrates the clear interdependence of class and sexual oppression, and also demonstrates (like *The Amazing Equal Pay Show*) the way that men and women who may share a general class interest are still divided by a sexist ideology that produces male chauvinism in men and passivity in women. However, since the group was mixed the political message is more evenly balanced: paralleling the 'lessons' Helen learns about work, trade unions and organised struggle are the 'lessons' that Dave learns about sharing equally in housework and looking after his children. The play tackles the division of labour at home and at work again with a mixture of naturalism and theatrical and visual imagery. The main 'story' is naturalistic, and the polemic points are made through satire (a 'time and motion study' man wears huge clock faces as spectacles) and through theatrical metaphor. One such metaphor became well known in political theatre: a discussion about the relationship between the concepts of parity and equal pay is illustrated in a scene in a pub, where the men order pints of beer and the women are expected to order half-pints. At the end of the scene Helen wraps up the discussion when she is asked what she wants to drink by saying that this time she'll have a pint. It was a moment when theatrical image and polemical point came together simply and effectively – not something which is easy to achieve in most agitprop theatre.

Conclusions

The plays described above were not, of course, the only ones to show the impact of sexual politics; there were others produced on the 'fringe' during the same period. For example, Sidewalk theatre company did a show called *Rainy Day Women* in 1969, described as 'how man made supergirl 1969', and after the second Miss World demonstration I wrote a play called *The Day After Yesterday* which was performed at 1972 at the Act Inn, one of the many pub lunchtime theatres which were opening in London.

But these early feminist plays shared a number of features: firstly, the concern with the politics, with the 'message' of the plays. This involved a concern for the quality of communication between performers and audience – since at this stage in touring political theatre it was customary to follow plays with discussions. And this concern produced an interesting stylistic mix: the plays' message (generally about the lives and political consciousness of the working-class characters) was conveyed through naturalistic detail, and elements in the argument (particularly about the capitalist oppressors) were presented with extravagant, exaggerated imagery. Although this often produced a theatrical crudity, it already had slightly different consequences when sexual-political subject matter was at stake. Most importantly the home and family relationships were shown as a site of political struggle in themselves, integrally bound to the political struggle which takes place at work. The family in these plays (they are overwhelmingly about heterosexual relationships) is not a place of retreat where the fighting man goes home to the little woman, nor is it simply a backdrop for action – men having their union meeting at home, for example. In both the agitprop work and the 'art theatre' work of this time, women were central initiators of the action. The objects of strong criticism were those social pressures which held women back from action in life – the passivity of sexual objectification, and the confinement of home and family. 'Liberation' was not seen as a rejection of family life, but a spur to transform it, by re-examining the role of women, and by extension, that of men. Feminist agitprop brought together public and private (epic and domestic) struggles in a new way.

Gay theatre did not take off so confidently in these early years; for women to place themselves at the centre of stage action was to some extent working in the dark, with no received tradition of political plays about women to draw on. Some of the early, celebratory, gay street theatre brought the theatricality of certain aspects of gay life out into the public eye; in particular transvestism, a symbol of the assertion by gay men that they have the right to be 'feminine' or even 'effeminate', to counter assumptions about a repressive masculinity. But this was very controversial. Whereas the men claimed that 'It exposes the myth of womanhood. . . . It shows that anyone can do it', lesbians objected, seeing it as an unconscious reproduction of the misogyny inherent in the domi-nant sexual culture:

> It's a projection of the male view of women, the objectification of women. Men put on the clothes because they think they can 'be' women for a bit. But they can always take them off again.
>
> (*7 Days*, 1 December 1971)

Organisationally the feminist or feminist-influenced groups were working in a growing socialist theatre movement and they carried with them many of the same working principles – a belief in demystifying theatrical skills, sharing the work and responsibility collectively, and dispensing with writers, directors, etc. Theatre subsidy at this stage was not a firmly established component in alternative theatre life, and in any case the prevailing anti-authori-tarian ethos was positively anti-professional in some quarters. Political conviction, having a good time, expressing one's creativity and spreading the word of revolution were all seen as part of the same process. The consequences were sometimes crude, sometimes oppressive, but often vivid and spontaneous. For women who had always experienced themselves as secondary in public events, this libertarianism was very important. The mixture of anger, exuber-ance and the discovery of new liberated energies challenged the boundaries of both politics and theatre:

The show was an ambitious multi-dimensional affair, with dance, song, drama, tape/slides and paintings. . . . The walls were adorned with collages of advertisements and magazine cuttings aimed at, and degrading to, women as well as a washing-line laden with nappies. It was clearly more than a show; we were bombarding our audience with our lot . . . it began with a sketch parodying women's role in marriage (Holy Padlock), using a show-dummy as the bride . . . lots of poetry . . . blues singers . . . and ten of us closed the show singing a Liberation song dressed in a huge ten-headed T-shirt. . . . We did manage to convey, fairly forcibly, a sense of the joy and excitement of women being together, which is something most people outside the Women's Movement have seen little of.

(Helen Taylor, writing about *Sistershow*, an event in Bristol,
Spare Rib, June 1973)

4

The second phase: 1973–7

The first Women's Theatre Festival

In the spring of 1973 a woman involved in a mixed media group was looking for a theatre to host a series of events; in the course of her search she discovered that the Almost Free Theatre, run by the community arts venture, Inter-Action, was free the following autumn. After a series of meetings with other women (both professionals and non-professionals) interested in theatre, the idea of setting up a Women's Theatre Festival was conceived. During that summer over a hundred women came to workshops, readings and discussions, and eventually a ten-week programme of lunch-time plays was planned. There was difficulty over the choice of plays, not only from within the group, but because Ed Berman, artistic director of the theatre, insisted on having a final say on selection, even though he was in all other respects prepared to hand over the season to the group, with skeletal (if invaluable) help from Inter-Action staff.

The group called itself the Women's Theatre Group (WTG); it attracted a wide range of women – professional theatre women who had little interest in feminism but were frustrated at the lack of work, and thought there might be something going; women who had done feminist street theatre; professionals who were also feminists; and women who were attracted to using theatre either as self-expression or as a vehicle for political propaganda. Inevitably, with the time to plan a season, both theoretical and practical differences arose, as would be the case with any cultural work seeking to combine political and aesthetic intentions. Questions basic to the whole concept of 'political theatre' were being tested throughout the season: if the political message is right, does the art matter? Can the politics only be effectively conveyed if the standard of theatrical expertise is high? Can anyone do theatre, or is it the province of the professionals? And how do people who feel strongly about different aspects of these arguments work together in the interests of theatre and the position of women?

Although some women faded from the planning group, in the event the season was exciting and varied, and it drew a lot of interest. It was written, directed, designed and stage-managed by women, although there were men performers in some of the plays. The season also included exhibitions, talks, workshops and a crèche during performances. The concluding paragraph of the first press release tried to reconcile differing views of the political function of theatre, and placed its major emphasis on the shared need for support and mutual encouragement:

> The Festival is designed to display the viability, competence and capability of women as a vital and necessary force within theatre. The WTG hopes to provide not only a platform but also an atmosphere of creative understanding and impetus. The Group is dependent on the responsible participation and mutual support of all its members and the expertise each can contribute. In this way we hope to exchange skills and acquire new talents while developing a group of interchangeable people to work together at a high level of professionalism.

The four lunchtime programmes consisted of *Instrument for Love* by Jennifer Phillips, directed by Liane Aukin, a satire about high culture and sexual game playing; *The Amiable Courtship of Miz Venus and Wild Bill* by Pam Gems, directed by Caroline Eves, a hard-edged farce satirising the twin extremes of sexually-obsessed men and man-hating women; a triple bill directed by Midge Mackenzie, consisting of *Love Food* by Dinah Brooke, about violent family relationships, *Crabs* by American writer Sally Ordway, a revue sketch about a 'liberated' couple, and my own *Mal de Mère* about a mother-daughter relationship; lastly, *Parade of Cats* by Jane Wibberley, directed by Susan Todd, about a cavalcade of varying female 'types'.

The season solicited and attracted attention from the press, ranging from a receptive and sympathetic article in *Time Out* (written by a woman, Naseem Khan) through the timorous John Barber in the *Daily Telegraph* (9 October 1973): 'I went along expecting an aggressively feminist point of view and rather dreading it' to the prejudiced relief of the anonymous critic in the *Kensington Post* (29 December 1973): 'Women's Theatre Festival did the valuable service of showing a mixed audience that females can laugh at themselves and are capable of amusement as well as awareness.' But perhaps more important than this challenge to the prejudices of male theatre critics was the fact that for the first time feminism and theatre had confronted each other directly. Street theatre and touring agitprop were at this stage self-selectedly outside the professional system, with politics and vivid self-expression as priorities. Because the season took place in a theatre building, as part of the professional fringe, new questions inevitably arose about the relationship between politics and art, and the position of women within the theatre industry itself.

The Women's Company

There was no doubt at the end of the season that there was great enthusiasm and scope for more work to be done; the questions were about the direction in which the work was to go. In early 1974 a group of women from the season produced a short play about abortion, and then did a dramatised reading of selections from *The Three Marias*, a book by three Portuguese women who were currently being tried for their feminist and anti-Catholic views. There was then a decisive split reflecting (although not always clearly) a complementary division of interest.

One half called itself the Women's Company, and included men. In their first press release they defined their aims:

> The women in this Company have many years' experience in the theatrical profession and are committed to creating greater opportunity for women throughout theatre. . . .
> While we intend at all times to present feminist theatre we do not wish to deal in diatribe. Our aim is to illustrate our

position by entertainment which is at the same time good
enough to create a new awareness of and help to correct the
inequalities within a profession falsely rumoured to be
egalitarian.

There is here both a defensive uncertainty about what might be
the general relationship between politics and art (an assumption
that feminism can only be expressed through diatribe – usually an
accusation lobbed from the misogynist camp), and a militancy
towards the position of women within the industry itself. Feminist
theatre is not defined, except by possible implication, as some kind
of entertaining theatre about women.

The Women's Company, as a flexible group of professional
theatre workers, run by women, mounted only two productions:
the first was *Go West, Young Woman*, written in about a week
by Pam Gems and staged in the Roundhouse in London in May
1974. It was an ambitious, sprawling musical about the distaff side
of pioneering life in America, with music and songs. The other
production was *My Name is Rosa Luxemburg*, by French writer
Marianne Auricoste, translated by Pam Gems, a lunchtime
production in early 1976 at the Soho Poly theatre in London. Both
productions were directed by Susan Todd. At different times the
group made efforts to base themselves in a permanent theatre, and
to get Arts Council subsidy; the fact that they failed to cohere may
be partly to do with chance, partly because of the wide range of
professional/political allegiances within the group; some women
were self-proclaimed feminists, others cautious about allying themselves with feminism. But the failure to cohere must also be seen
to emerge from the objective situation. As a group of women's
voices within the profession (let alone a group of feminist voices),
they were isolated and went virtually unheard. No one had as yet
vociferously challenged the position of women in the industry, and
as individuals dropped out of the group to take freelance jobs the
impetus behind the Women's Company faded.

The Women's Theatre Group

The other half of the original group retained the name of the Women's Theatre Group. Their first press release declared an explicit allegiance to feminism, declaring that their work was:

> directed towards exploration of the female situation from a feminist viewpoint. It aims also at increasing understanding of the political and social context in which women operate. . . . Our group, as a by-product of the Women's Movement, has always functioned in a totally collective manner, trying to avoid leadership and hierarchies. Apart from the difficulties of functioning without any subsidy whatsoever, one of our most acute problems has been attempting to combine politics and polemic with aesthetics and entertainment.

Political content and more democratic ways of working, drawing a clear parallel between political and artistic working methods, took precedence over a concern for the position of women in the theatre industry. The Group saw its work as outgoing and propagandist, rather than as a means by which to encourage the creativity of women for its own sake, although they too were concerned about the relationship between politics and aesthetics. The Women's Theatre Group were more advantaged in that their work already had a context (unlike that of the Women's Company) – that of the socialist touring network, and there was some general precedent for what they were doing. At least two of the women who comprised the new Women's Theatre Group complement of seven had had previous experience in community and touring theatre.

The Group's first piece of work was *Fantasia*, a collectively devised and written piece about women's fantasies, performed at a number of London fringe venues. The Group then formulated a policy which was to remain the cornerstone of their work for some time: devising and taking plays to teenagers. This involved a careful and painstaking campaign to find their own audiences, contacting teachers, youth club and community workers, as well as performing sometimes in small theatre venues to politically sympathetic audiences.

Their first play was *My Mother Says*,[1] a group-devised piece about sex and contraception for 15- to 18-year-olds. Two 15-year-old girls are about to leave school; at an all-night party one of them has her first sexual experience and afterwards is afraid she is pregnant. She turns out not to be, but the 'story' enables the audience to see her relationship with other women in her family – fearful, puritan Mum and the more 'liberated', carefree Granny – and their differing attitudes to sex. The play also shows the importance of solidarity and support from other women (the girl's friends, a sympathetic gynaecologist), and argues overall for a more open and liberal approach to heterosexual experience for women. Punctuated with songs, it was a simple, modern morality play, conveying factual information about contraception. The play toured during 1975.

Work to Role (1976) followed one of the girls from the first play after she leaves school to find a job. Again the play put emphasis on the importance of communication and solidarity between women, demonstrating a range of political positions – an older woman with years of trade union militancy behind her and a younger woman with no patience with male-dominated unions. The play concentrated on showing two particularly exploited areas of 'women's work' – catering and casual secretarial jobs.

The third play, *Out! On the Costa del Trico* (1977), was based on an industrial dispute about equal pay at a London firm making windscreen wipers. It was a topical piece, involving the group in a current political issue and in branching out to adult audiences. Four hundred women factory workers were claiming equal pay with a handful of men who were doing the same work but being paid more. The women picketed the factory during the hot summer of 1976 (hence the title – part of the banter of the picketing women), and they were supported by feminists and by trade unionists all over London. The real life situation reflected the same problem as had been demonstrated in *The Amazing Equal Pay Show* – some of the women had to face hostility from their husbands simply because they were taking independent action, illustrating the way sexism produces divisions within classes. The play's form again followed the formula of a naturalistic story framed by entertaining devices; at the same time it demonstrated in greater detail the complexities and loopholes in the Equal Pay Act. The songs were witty pastiches on pulp-pop numbers.

Gay Sweatshop

Following the success of the Women's Theatre Festival, Ed Berman put out an open invitation in the summer of 1974 for gay theatre workers to organise a similar season. The initial responses came from men, and as with the women's season, Ed Berman had final say in the choice of plays. The group decided that all writers and directors must be gay, but were less stringent about performers: two of the plays also had women characters.

The gay season ran at lunchtime from March to May 1975; the first play was *Limitations* by John Roman Baker, about a gay man who leaves his lover to go and live with a woman because he wants a child; next came *Thinking Straight* by Laurence Collinson, directed by Drew Griffiths, about the self-censorship in art and life which gay men experience; the third programme was *Ships* by Alan Wakeman, directed by Gerald Chapman, three short plays on the obstacles which prevent the sense of a gay identity. After that came *One Person*, a monologue spoken by a gay man to his lover, and *Fred and Harold*, two men trying to negotiate the basis for a gay relationship. Both plays were by Robert Patrick, directed by Stewart Trotter. The final play in the season was *Passing By* by Martin Sherman, a bittersweet love story about two men. Running concurrently with the lunchtime production was an evening play by Robert Patrick, *The Haunted Host*, directed by John Chapman, a two-hander in which a gay man, whose lover has committed suicide, is visited by a young, bigoted, male heterosexual.

In some ways the plays were all more 'literary' than their counterparts in the women's season; a higher proportion of the men taking part in the gay season were sophisticated professionals, and for them part of the challenge was to fellow workers whom they knew to be gay to 'come out' and change their attitudes. The problem was clearly put in Roger Baker's introduction to a book which published most of the plays from this season (the women's plays were not similarly published):

No sense of gay identification has emerged from the theatre, be it mainstream, fringe or experimental. Yet, traditionally the theatre is supposed to employ a higher percentage of homosexuals than any other profession. Members of Gay Sweatshop who have approached professional actors and directors have met with responses ranging from guarded interest to downright terror. . . . Audiences are invited to deride gays. But audiences include homosexuals as well, and they too will willingly enter into the complicity and go armoured to withstand the barbs and grotesque parodies of themselves.

(*Homosexual Acts*, Inter-Action, 1975, pp. vi–vii)

A play about coming out as a lesbian, *Any Woman Can* by Jill Posener, had been turned down by Ed Berman on the grounds that it wasn't 'theatrical' enough. The produced plays, then, focused explicitly on male adult homosexual relationships, outside any kind of family context, questioning almost without exception the need for monogamy and the stereotypical basis of heterosexual relationships. Many of the plays were poised between the tragedy and the potential of living openly as a homosexual, and only *Thinking Straight* ended with a clear polemical 'come out' message to the audience.

The name 'Gay Sweatshop' had evolved during the season, which acted as a catalyst for the group. They continued almost immediately with their first group show, *Mr X*, written by Drew Griffiths and Roger Baker. This play followed the experience and changing consciousness of one man, from early attempts to make him into a woman-hating heterosexual, through a series of encounters with closet gays, into joining GLF and 'coming out' in a simple speech to the audience at the end. Although most of the men drawn to the Almost Free season were already professional theatre people, some had been involved in the Gay Liberation Front and brought with them a more analytical understanding of homosexual oppression. *Mr X* reflected that polemical bias. The play toured the country during 1975, and the men were often challenged by women in the audience who said they couldn't call themselves a gay theatre group if they had no women in the company.

The success of the tour encouraged Gay Sweatshop to organise a second season of gay plays during 1976, at the Institute of

Contemporary Arts in London. *Any Woman Can* was included, having been performed for one night at a Women's Theatre Festival at the Haymarket Theatre in Leicester in the autumn of 1975. The title expressed the simple message of the play; like *Mr X* it was an episodic parable of a gay person's acceptance and pride in her homosexuality. But it was also full of accounts of the contradictions and prejudices which any lesbian must face, as well as her own internalised uncertainties. The season also included *Stone* by Edward Bond, written at the invitation of Gay Sweatshop and not dealing with homosexuality at all; it was an allegory about the burdens (the 'stone') which the oppressed carry round with them, and in the context of the season was controversial, as some members of the Company felt it had only been solicited to draw public attention to the season. There was also *Indiscreet*, a sort of follow-up to *Mr X*, by Roger Baker and Drew Griffiths, *The Fork* by Ian Brown and *Randy Robinson's Unsuitable Relationship* by Andrew Davies.

The Company was now mixed and the men and women worked on two shows together: *Jingle Ball* (1976), a pantomime spoof on Cinderella in which the Prince and Cinders are played by women who fall in love, though the Ugly Sisters were played by men just as in the conventional panto. The style of the piece was interesting because it combined different theatrical and political approaches, which were later one of the reasons for the men and women splitting into two groups. The actors playing the Ugly Sisters did so with a full awareness of the male theatrical camp tradition, sending up its reactionary aspects (the anti-women and anti-gay jokes that so often are part of pantomime banter) while enjoying to the full the absurdities of playing with extravagant sexual behaviour. The Prince and Cinders, on the other hand, were played 'straight', with a gentle twist in that the true love was lesbian rather than heterosexual.

In the early part of 1977 the men and women worked together on *Age of Consent*, a play which was presented at the Royal Court Theatre as part of the Young People's Theatre Scheme, which explored the relationship of the law to homosexuality (between consenting adults over 21), and its effect on relationships.

During 1977 the Company split into a men's and a women's group, each with artistic autonomy, but working under the same

gay issues
vs
feminist
issues

sexuality
vs.

gender

sexism vs.
homophobia

56   The second phase: 1973–7

administrative umbrella. This was for two reasons: the first was similar to the split that had occurred within the Gay Liberation Front itself, in that lesbians felt that many features of their oppression were shared more with other women than with gay men. One of the consequences of this was to be seen in a conflict between theatrical styles, in that the men drew on an already familiar camp and drag tradition, which they both celebrated and tried to stand on its head, whereas the women leaned more towards the newer agitprop, documentary-based styles, as a means of showing hitherto suppressed experience as it really is. The problem of male dominance in the organisation of the group and the clash of styles was acknowledged on both sides, and the plays done in 1977 reflected this divergence of emphasis.

As Time Goes By[2] by Noel Greig and Drew Griffiths, the men's play, consisted of sections which dramatised the overt repression of homosexuals – the Oscar Wilde trial and after, Berlin in the 1930s, ending in 1969, with the stirrings of the new Gay Liberation Movement in America. The women's group took the cue for their next play from suggestions by members of audiences: there had recently been a number of custody cases in which the courts made adverse comments or passed judgements against lesbian mothers. The play thus stemmed from a desire to intervene in a political 'issue', to defend the right to motherhood of women who had become lesbians and who were being censured by the State. During the research period, the company came to see the State's attitude to lesbian mothers as symptomatic of attitudes to all mothers if they transgress the assumed norms of wife and motherhood. Although the company's intention was to research, improvise and then write the play collectively, when they had planned the story and structured the play, they asked me to script the material they had gathered. The play was interesting for the links it made between a lesbian 'issue' and a wider feminist critique, demonstrating the way that the official views about family and sexual morality intrude into ordinary life. The style of the play reflected this – the first half naturalistic snatches of three different women's lives, the second half a stylised montage based on transcripts of the hearings of two of the cases. Care and Control[3] remains one of the few plays about contemporary sexual politics which has dealt directly with the role and authority of the State in personal and sexual life.

Monstrous Regiment

By 1976 both the Women's Theatre Group and Gay Sweatshop were firmly established, although neither was yet a full-time company on a revenue grant from the Arts Council. Both were touring groups; in other parts of the country all-women's groups and other gay theatre groups formed, and in some mixed socialist groups women performers were beginning to question the male bias in terms of both numbers and content. The presence of the above two groups, whose approach was clearly defined in terms of sexual politics, enabled other theatre workers to question their own situation, generating a snowball effect within the regional arts theatres and the alternative theatre movement itself.

One such response was the Women's Theatre Festival held at the Haymarket Theatre, Leicester, in the autumn of 1975. As well as Jill Posener's play, *Any Woman Can*, there was lunchtime, evening, and late-night theatre by women: plays by Olwen Wymark, Pam Gems, Caryl Churchill, Jennifer Phillips, Dinah Brooke, Liane Aukin and myself. As an event which asserted its links with politics, it also included talks, readings, discussions and music.

This slow diffusion of gay and feminist consciousness led to the formation of a new group. During the summer of 1975 performer Gillian Hanna was with Belt and Braces theatre group in a play with only two women's parts. She was cast in one and the group auditioned for another woman. She was struck by the energy and abilities of the women who auditioned, and as a result of the contacts she made, a small group of women performers met during the summer, discussing, among other things, the relatively raw deal they had in fringe and political plays. They decided to start a new group, which was named Monstrous Regiment, taken from the title of the misogynist, sixteenth-century pamphlet by John Knox. The group was to include men, and an early press release defined their aim of reversing the conventional balance of power between the sexes:

> The company . . . ensures that women form the majority and
> take on decisive roles, and also commissions work by
> women writers dealing with themes throwing light on the
> position of society . . .

Another press release amplified:

> We see ourselves as part of the growing and lively movement
> to improve the status of women. Our work explores the
> experience of women past and present, and we want to place
> that experience in the centre of the stage, instead of in the
> wings.

In the original impetus behind the group, there are clear links
with the Women's Company – a basic concern to enhance the
role of women in theatre, both onstage and off, and a cautious
recognition of their relationship to feminism. But there were also
important differences: firstly, the cultural context had changed,
and sexual politics was now permeating some areas of alternative
theatre. Secondly, the women all had some years of experience
in fringe theatre and socialist theatre groups, and had a wider
understanding of the problems for women in radical theatre. But,
like the Women's Company, they were interested in playing the
art theatre circuit, rather than going out to new audiences as
the Women's Theatre Group had done. Also like the Women's
Company, they were concerned to intervene in theatrical work,
drawing on fairly high levels of artistic skill, and their early work
included a concern for the function of music in theatre in its own
right, rather than simply as light relief, leavening the political
message, or back-up to the written text.

For their first four shows the performing group consisted of five
women and two men, and the administration was done by women.
As a performer-managed group, all management decisions were
collectively made, but there was no initial interest in devising shows
collectively, or following through the experiments in breaking
down the division of labour throughout the production process. In
describing the origins of the group, Gillian Hanna later said that
'feminism overtook us' (interview with the author, 1980); and in
the group's developing policy and the impact of their plays the
uneven relationship between politics and theatrical expertise was

Monstrous Regiment

reflected. At one level their early aims were ambitious and new: they sought to explore male/female relations, but did so inadequately, in a group where men were in the minority. They were also excited by the possibility of reclaiming the history play from women's point of view, and their first play was commissioned from a husband and wife team, C. G. Bond and Claire Luckham. The company reworked parts of the script, and *Scum: Death, Destruction and Dirty Washing*, directed by Susan Todd, was first performed during the summer of 1976. It was set largely in a laundry (i.e., on female social territory) in Paris during 1870–1, when the people of Paris briefly declared self-government in the Paris Commune.

The core of the play showed the women being affected by surrounding political events, and deciding to take control of their own lives and work, by taking over the laundry. Inevitably this involved some exploration of the relationship between the working-class women and political power – both bourgeois and revolutionary. The laundry workers had their own struggle – developing confidence and understanding among themselves, and then throwing their woman boss out – but they had little direct contact with the militants fighting in the streets. This point – about how ordinary women are cut off from public struggles – was made in a series of monologues spoken by a French bourgeoise about what was happening at the seat of the besieged government at Versailles. The role of men in the play was secondary; the action emphasised the relationships between the women.

Later in 1976 Monstrous Regiment staged *Vinegar Tom*, written by Caryl Churchill, and directed by a guest director, Pam Brighton. Set in the seventeenth century the play looked at men, women and witchcraft, weaving a complex, taut account of the web of fear, faith, ignorance and superstition which was the breeding-ground for witch-hunting. The play showed in particular how women's sexuality was feared and hated and blamed for all kinds of social ills. The group's third play was written by company member Susan Todd and performer/director Ann Mitchell. *Kiss and Kill*, which toured through 1977, was set in the present, a series of sketched portraits on the theme of violence, ranging from the experience of an American soldier in Vietnam, to a woman receiving obscene phone-calls from her ex-husband.

In all three plays music played an important role; in *Scum* the songs were mood-music pieces, enhancing dramatic moments in the play. In the next two plays music was used differently, to create its own dimension of meaning. In *Kiss and Kill* spare drum-and-voice motifs punctuated the scenes, and in *Vinegar Tom* something more ambitious was attempted. Cast members punctuated the historical play by appearing in modern dress, singing songs specially written to draw parallels between the historic phenomenon of witchcraft and present day attitudes to women. It was also a device which was meant to reflect the relationship of the performers to their product – to show that women of today can make use of and learn from the struggles and solidarities of women in the past. Politically it had the effect of drawing an oversimplistic parallel between seventeenth- and twentieth-century women. In *Kiss and Kill* the play's structure was rambling and fragmented, supposedly reflecting the way women experience their lives as dislocated and fragmented; it was stronger in its individual moments than its overall impact, and it is important to note that it was only in this third play that the development of a real company hand in the plays began. The first two plays had been commissioned from established writers outside the group who had had little direct contact with feminism. Having begun by establishing a women-dominated group with a sound theatrical reputation, Monstrous Regiment then approached the direct matter of the relationship between their own political consciousnesses as women and the product onstage.

Conclusions

The increases in Arts Council subsidy during the first part of this period helped the expansion of alternative theatre. Individuals were beginning to find or form theatre groups in which their concerns as women or gays could be represented. The four strands which provided the source of gay and (particularly) feminist energy expanded and overlapped; individuals moved from university or Theatre-in-Education groups into political touring companies, or into one of the many fringe theatres. This cross-fertilisation helped develop a greater diversity of work, in terms of audience, political content and theatrical forms all over the country. In London a Feminist Theatre Study Group began meeting in 1976, open to women (and, at first, to sympathetic men) working in theatre; the group acted as a discussion forum and during 1977 campaigned for the reconvening of a Women's Sub-Committee within Equity – which they achieved in 1978.

The middle of the 1970s also saw the presence of a small number of women in the upper echelons of prestige subsidised theatre: Caryl Churchill's *Objections to Sex and Violence* was staged at the Royal Court in 1975, and she worked with Monstrous Regiment and Joint Stock theatre group the following year. Pam Gems (who had been associated with the Women's Company) had a play called *Dead Fish* produced at the Edinburgh Festival in autumn 1976; the following year the play reappeared to general critical praise at the Hampstead Theatre Club, now entitled *Dusa, Fish, Stas and Vi*, and transferred to the Mayfair Theatre. Her *Queen Christina* was produced at The Other Place, the Royal Shakespeare Company's studio theatre in Stratford, also in autumn 1977. In the mid-1970s Buzz Goodbody, the only woman director to be on the RSC's staff, who had herself been instrumental in the opening of The Other Place, directed two impressive experimental productions of *King Lear* (1974) and *Hamlet* (1975) before her tragic suicide just after the opening of the latter. In the autumn of 1977 Kate Crutchley and Nancy Diuguid, who had worked with Gay Sweatshop, initiated another multi-media festival – Women's Festival '77 at the Drill Hall in London – at which *Voices*, a poetic play by American feminist, Susan Griffin, was performed. Following the success of this festival, men from Gay Sweatshop initiated a *Gay Times Festival*, a London-based arts event, which has recurred since.

The three groups whose work has been described in some detail represent different emphases on the political theatre axis, reflected in their audiences, their ways of working, the class content of their work, and the theatrical forms they took on and explored. The Women's Theatre Group continued feminist agitprop work, refining its format, carrying through its didactic purpose in discussions after performances, researching and devising collectively, and in their form combining the naturalistic storyline (consciously chosen as a form popularised by television drama)

Socialist - Feminist approach: The Women's Theatre Group

with the more theatrical devices of pastiche and song. The class content (and consciousness-raising aim) of their work concentrated on the statistical majority, the average, 'typical' experience of the working-class woman – the girls who leave school with few qualifications, the women working in the least organised, unskilled and semi-skilled areas of work. As an all-women's group they represented class struggle from the base line of female territory, critical of sexist male attitudes, but not often attacking men as such, merely excluding them from the immediate scope of the action. They emphasised the need for solidarity and communication between women, but indicated that women can be divided by different class interests. This broad socialist-feminist approach combined neatly with the didactic intention of presenting the audience with a series of arguments and leaving it to discussions to crystallise actual views.

The formal consequences of this broad socialist-feminist approach to the experience of woman was double-edged: it produced character 'types', the personification of predetermined political positions, or representatives of an argument, rather than the more fully developed notion of the contradictory individual 'character'. But this very lack of theatrical sophistication itself makes a polemical point and introduces a new content – placing the individual woman in her social and political context, and presenting the feminist idea of the developing consciousness of woman from a passive acceptance of her situation to a desire to change it. And the very all-femaleness of the stage world continually reminds us how rare an event it is to see a play about women in a society where female association is still discouraged or trivialised, where 'women's talk' is a derogatory term. These plays are essentially polemical entertainment on the situation of contemporary women. This period of their work straddled the audiences covered by Theatre-in-Education and adult agitprop, in a context where feedback from these audiences was important for their future credibility.

Monstrous Regiment's work was more conventionally aimed at the touring theatre circuit, with no immediate didactic purpose and no discussions. The nature of their work was at one level more ambitious than that of the Women's Theatre Group; they pitched their artistic standards high, commissioned established writers (at first) and included men in a minority in the group, while wishing to show the reality of male-female relationships. One of the merits of their first two plays was to reclaim the history play from male domination by reinterpreting important historic events from the women's angle. Where the Women's Theatre Group came to its aesthetic conclusions from its political views and intentions, having begun with conscious links with the Women's Liberation Movement, Monstrous Regiment began from a more simplified pro-woman position, perhaps a more intuitive approach to the position of women. However, because of their desire to establish a secure professional reputation on the art-theatre circuit, they were able to commission work from experienced writers which, after discussion and further work from the company, produced a more subtle demonstration of the possibilities of cross-class female solidarity.

In *Scum* a young middle-class woman joins the workers, teaching them to read and write; in *Vinegar Tom* the attitude of the authorities to peasant and gentry women is shown to be subtly different – whereas the peasant women are controlled by brute force, the local landowner's daughter is controlled by being diagnosed as ill or mad. However, Monstrous Regiment also had men in the group, in the interests of showing the world 'as it really is'. In the event men acted in supporting roles, reversing the usual pattern of dominance in plays. If their intention was to try to tackle sexual politics from both the male and female ends of the experience, these early plays failed, although the fact of reversing the supporting roles itself made an implicit polemical point about the audience's other theatrical experiences.

The Women's Theatre Group and Monstrous Regiment concentrated on the female heterosexual experience, and on placing groups of women (rather than individual 'heroines') in their social and political context. Their women characters were placed in critically viewed family relationships (the mother and daughter in *Vinegar Tom*, a particularly poignant and strong relationship). *Care and Control*, the women's Gay Sweatshop play, dealt with motherhood under attack. The Gay Sweatshop men's plays, however, dealt with the individual adult male, free of familial ties, exploring sexual liberation and the freedom to break through the boundaries of masculine/feminine sexual stereotypes. The men's plays on the whole confronted sexuality more directly than the women's plays, reflecting both the greater historical presence of gay men's social subculture, but also reflecting the fact that parenthood is not a direct option for individual men, and consequently some aspects of gay men's sexual culture place greater emphasis on casual and passing sexual relationships.

There was also a class difference between the men's and the women's work in Gay Sweatshop: the men's work tended to present the struggle of homosexuals in terms of developing individual courage to 'come out', and to draw on their own history and semi-bohemian, middle-class lifestyles. The women, perhaps because their political sympathies were closer to feminism than to male gay oppression, tended to reflect the concerns of agitprop feminism and to focus on working-class lesbian experience. Their work also represented women who chose relationships or motherhood as well as 'single' women, opting for a different kind of independence. But both the men's and the women's work, despite these differences, shared the polemical purpose of presenting gay experience with pride and encouraging other homosexuals by their example to find the courage to 'come out', to cease concealing their sexuality.

5

The third phase: from 1977

The Women's Theatre Group: agitprop and after

The year 1977 was in some ways a turning point for the Women's Theatre Group. During that year they produced two plays in line with their earlier policy: *Pretty Ugly* and *In Our Way*, both group written. The first was a youth show about the effect of fashion images; the second an adult show exploring the effect of sex discrimination legislation on women workers, in a factory and in journalism. However, the climate of fervour for simple agitprop work was changing, and members of the group were also somewhat dissatisfied with the pressures imposed by a scrupulous adherence to the anyone-can-do-anything approach. They employed freelance women directors and designers for these shows, and a two-tier policy of one youth and one adult show each year was established.

During 1978 they also decided to employ writers for the first time, and commissioned *Hot Spot* from Eileen Fairweather and Melissa Murray (who the previous year had written and performed *Bouncing Back with Benyon*, a satire on the anti-abortion lobby who were threatening to pass Parliamentary measures to reduce women's access to abortion). None of these three Women's Theatre Group plays had the artistic precision or political bite of the group's early work: in part because the climate had changed and early enthusiasm had settled; in part because the changing composition of the group inevitably altered the nature of the debates; and in part because the group was also changing its methods of work. During 1979 they commissioned two more plays from women writers – an adult show, *Soap Opera* by American writer Donna

Franceschild, about a group of women who are accidentally locked in a laundrette, and a youth show, *The Wild Bunch* by Bryony Lavery, about girls in a youth club. Again, both shows had little overt political dynamism about them, concentrating more on women's day-to-day relationships with each other. But this in itself was a rather important new departure. Instead of placing dramatic events at a point in women's lives where political action, or at the very least, political understanding, was demanded of them, these two plays were about the far more ordinary, everyday events that can happen to young and older women.

In *Soap Opera* the device of the women being accidentally locked in the laundrette (a man has the key) means that there is an opportunity to observe and hear about the women's lives. In a sense this play – like a number of others being performed by other groups – was an example of the principle of consciousness-raising onstage, a naturalistic laying-out of the territory of day-to-day experience, rather than calling for, or demonstrating, the importance of political activism. The play was punctuated by powerful rock songs, in which each woman, musical-style, could express what she was 'really' feeling. The irony was that the play remained at the level of its own sense of hermeticism, and the women were only 'freed' when the man with the key arrived to let them out of the room. The very safety within which the women had got to know each other better was revealed as in the power of a man.

During the first part of 1980 the group produced two shows – a co-devised anthology of writer Stevie Smith's work, *Better a Live Pompey Than a Dead Cyril* and *My Mkinga* about drug dumping in the third world, co-researched and devised by director Julie Holledge and writer Kate Phelps and written by the latter.

These two plays marked another change in the group's work: an interest in the cultural history of women through writing, and in the exploitation of third world people by medical research. Until now all the group's work had been topical, immediate and about urban British female experience. The group's next two plays were written by Timberlake Wertenbaker; the first, *Breaking Through* (1980), was a rather awkward mixture of naive sci-fi and realistic material about the threat of nuclear power – a less naturalistic way of returning to an immediate contemporary concern as it affected women. Her other play, *New Anatomies*[1] (1981), was a more literary effort, concentrating on a demonstration of the way some nineteenth-century women adventurers dressed as men, 'in order to lead more interesting and creative lives' – a performance style that went some way towards a realistic, rather than strictly stylised, exploration of a kind of ideologically motivated cross-dressing.

Following that came *Time Pieces*[2] (1982), devised and scripted by the company and its director Lou Wakefield. The preoccupation with exploring women in history, which had marked some recent work, here became a very self-conscious subject matter, returning to a neat agitprop style, in a play where an aunt tells her young niece about the history of the women in her family by looking through an old photograph album. This gentle consciousness-raising exercise reconciles mother and daughter at the end of the play, and the show was punctuated by a mixture of songs, old and new.

The next play continued the mixture of company devising with the directorial support of Libby Mason in *Double Vision* (1982), a simple and moving two-hander which returned to women and contemporary politics by tracing the bittersweet political and sexual relationship between two young women. In 1983 writer Elizabeth Bond wrote *Love and Dissent*, in which the story of Russian Alexandra Kollontai (real life) was interwoven with the life of a fictional woman teacher, her political/work dilemmas, and her daughter. The mixture of past and present was awkwardly merged, and the play was caught between two uncomfortable alternatives: it was neither a historical play, nor was it a fully developed contemporary story. Perhaps the scheme itself had been overambitious, and the idea remained unrealised. Women's own records and comments on their history were the subject of *Dear Girl* (1983), devised by Tierl Thompson and director Libby Mason, and based on the letters and diaries of four women who lived at the turn of the century. The basic feminist principles of a particular kind of supportive friendship between women shone through a rather unwieldy and mechanically constructed script, which again hovered between two alternatives: half illustrated lecture, half dramatic reconstruction, with some very moving moments.

The two plays produced in 1984 were *Trade Secrets*, by Jacqui Shapiro and *Pax* by Deborah Levy, both young writers, and commissioning them was consistent with the group's avowed policy of encouraging new women writers, something which the Women's Theatre Group has supported through regular play-readings of new work. In their different ways, neither play really worked completely; in both, some inventive and surreal imaginations and wit were evident, but neither really found its own stylistic level. In a sense these are difficult comments to make on the work of young writers; but each production must stand on its own merits, and satisfy the people who go to see it. It is important to add the caveat that a company such as the Women's Theatre Group has to be supported when it takes such risks, and that one can approve of the risks and still have reservations about the product.

Gay Sweatshop and spin-offs

During 1978 Gay Sweatshop produced three shows: the women, following on the success of *Care and Control*, collectively devised and wrote *What the Hell is She Doing Here?*, a stylised series of sketches on coming out. The company was almost entirely new, and perhaps inevitably the play was more important as a means of self-expression for the company members, rather than a development in the work of Gay Sweatshop women, though the piece did contain a witty sketch about a women's centre, affectionately sending up some of the more absurd aspects of collective work. The second show was *Iceberg*, also collectively devised and written, and another attempt by the men and women to work together. Its form was revue-like; its subject was gays and fascism, and like earlier work by the men, incorporated historical references to male gay oppression, and drew a parallel between the individual courage needed to come out as homosexual and that needed to 'come out' against fascism. It also incorporated some interesting material on power – a confrontation between the men and the women, with the latter asserting that all men have power over women, the former asserting that they too were oppressed as gay men by macho virility. Again neither show took a clear class perspective, although in some ways this implicitly strengthened the 'come out' message as implying the complexity of cross-class struggles against sexual oppression and indirectly raising the question of the relationship between such 'ideological' struggles and those against material or economic exploitation. The third show was *Warm*, a show done by the men in cabaret style, based on the songs of Brecht and Weill, and looking at the situation of gay men in 1930s England and Germany, continuing an area of interest from *As Time Goes By*.

During 1979 Gay Sweatshop produced *The Dear Love of Comrades*,[3] by Noel Greig, about Edward Carpenter, the late nineteenth-century socialist and sexual radical. Carpenter tried to live out his belief that personal relationships and lifestyles had to change along with social and political institutions. The stage play was a carefully structured documentary, outlining Carpenter's political activism, and showing his artisan commune just outside Sheffield. The play interweaves history, polemic and the delicacy of a range of emotions, from romantic passion to jealousy; Carpenter's lifestyle involved relationships with three working-class men (all coincidentally called George (!)).

The play was all-male (although there were women involved in Carpenter's circle) and in this respect was true to the spirit of Carpenter's preoccupation with male 'fellowship'. The power of the play lies precisely in the fact that it focuses so clearly on the intensity of emotion and friendship between the men, and this demonstrates the kinds of strength, but from a male point of view, which some of the Women's Theatre Group work has carried. A play which fully-frontally (as it were) deals with members of one sex affords the writer and company a chance to explore a very full range of emotions between the members of that sex. The single-gendered play may be 'unrealistic' in the sense that we all inhabit a world which consists of men and women, but it does provide an imaginative opportunity to explore the nature of the gendered perspective (male or female) without the complexities and displacements of the 'mixed' play.

This is not a plea simply for a two-tier theatre, one of which explores male experience, and the other female experience – but a play such as *The Dear Love of Comrades* highlights the way in which, traditionally, emotional depth is only given to heterosexual relationships, and comradeship depth to relationships between heterosexual men. There remains a whole gamut of emotions and relationships between men and men, and women and women, sexual and non-sexual, which a play such as this can suggest. Noel

Greig and Drew Griffiths used the same source material about Edward Carpenter for a play which was transmitted by BBC Television, called *Only Connect*, which achieved a similar mix of emotional delicacy and a concern for gay men to reconstruct their history.

In 1979 there were two other shows: *I Like Me Like This*, by Sharon Nassaeur and Angela Stewart Park, a women's musical show, and *Who Knows*, by Sara Hardy, Bruce Bayley and Philip Timmins, who worked with a group of non-professional young people on a show about sexuality. During 1980 Angela Stewart Park and Noel Greig co-wrote a mixed company show about gender and reproduction, setting it in a futuristic society. The company's funding was then altered by the Arts Council; instead of being given an annual grant (as the Women's Theatre Group and Monstrous Regiment were) the company was relegated to having to apply for money for specific projects. This meant that company continuity was broken, and it wasn't until 1983 that the next Gay Sweatshop play was produced.

Poppies by Noel Greig was set simultaneously in 1939 and 1986; stylistically it combined the naturalistic story of the relationship between two men, with the surreal device of two 'Mouldy Heads', representing the subterranean, unspoken fears of death and decay. The imaginative power of the piece lay in the device of dramatic irony, whereby we, the audience, could see the continuing presence of the threat of death, and this worked on two distinct levels – the first, to suggest content parallels with the threat of nuclear extinction (linking the lives of gay people with the importance of the Peace Movement), and the second, to suggest a more delicate, individual knowledge which we all carry with us about the fear of our own death. The play had a second production during 1985.

Monstrous Regiment and sexuality

After *Kiss and Kill* Monstrous Regiment decided to concentrate more on their performance personae, particularly in the field of stand-up comedy, music-hall presentation and song, in line with many touring groups in the second half of the 1970s, who were similarly exploring popular entertainment forms. Monstrous Regiment were interested in working with cabaret-style performance, and exploring the sexual self-representation of the female performer and her relationship with her audience. Cabaret and stand-up comedy between them point up one way women are objectified: women as glamorous performers exude a high-society come-on which is then contained by a male-dominated humour in which there is often a collusive relationship between the male comic and the men in his audience at the expense of women. The distance of the audience from the desired object (the glamorous woman) is a crucial element in the conventional representation of glamour, which is a stylised symbol of dangerous (but tameable) female sexuality.

The women in the group wanted to explore the notion of glamour in the performance process, to show that women can be as funny as men, and, as individuals, to experiment with adlib exchanges with the audience. Their first production in 1977, *Floorshow*, was about women and work, with songs and sketches co-authored by Caryl Churchill, David Bradford, Bryony Lavery and myself. It included songs, monologues, sketches, comic patter about women and work in Africa, the idea of 'pin money', working as a bus conductor, reversed domestic roles, and the performers wore variegated, brightly coloured costumes – reminiscent of the variety of clown costumes, and with a bouncy uniformity which didn't make obvious sexual distinctions between the male and female performers. Their next cabaret, in 1978, *Time Gentlemen Please*, scripted by Bryony Lavery, was about sex, with a cast of three men and three women. The men's performances were muted: they wore dark, discreet suits, while the women ran exotic variations on the black and silver trappings of slinky cabaret costume. Songs and sketches were peppered with acute and often painful send-ups and perceptions about male and female sexual insecurities, competitiveness, romantic fantasies. The group toured, to a mixture of responses, including a performance in Leeds which was stopped by angry feminist and gay activists. In a correspondence about the show in the *Morning Star*, the Communist Party daily, criticisms were made of the:

'Glitter and glamour' and 'slinky silvery costumes' worn by the women of course, not the men. And identification galore for those of us who live in Chelsea flats and worry about whether the wine is at the right temperature for the dinner party. . . . It is also very undermining to be told that all these problems relating to sex can be overcome – just so long as they are sexually attractive, as self-assured and as middle-class as the women onstage. . . . Far from creating a Dietrich image in order to subvert it, Monstrous Regiment appears to indulge itself in the creation, to revel in the fantasy.

(letter from Sandra Hunt, 21 November 1978)

In a reply director Susan Todd defended the intention behind the show, claiming that the women performers

deconstruct their traditional mode of stage presence and abandon coyness, terror and self-doubt for a direct expression of sexuality. . . . That particular transformation was fought for very hard and it represents a victory for each woman over self-denigration.

(*Morning Star*, 28 November 1978)

The controversy revolved around questions central to the development of a new stage representation of female sexuality: it may have been new and courageous for those particular women as individuals to have developed a confident and glamorous stage presence, but they were doing so in a convention which already had a specific meaning for their audience – we are all familiar enough through television with the hard-edged challenge of female glamour. The fact that at one level the performances reinforced the very image they were hoping to undermine reflected both the strength of that dominant imagery and the failure of the material to provide content strong enough to rupture the form. The humour in the show was of two kinds – gentle satire and an aggressively sexual approach from the women. The latter could certainly have been interpreted as a 'liberated' come-on, with its effect a radical variant on the conventional female cabaret persona which divides the audience, inviting the men to possess and subdue her and the women to compete with her. Hence (perhaps inadvertently) the message produced a heterosexual 'radical' (as opposed to a socialist) feminism in which male dominance was replaced by female dominance, and the notion of a liberated female sexuality was not explored enough to take it beyond a counter image of woman as (trendy) castrator. It highlights the complexity of image and meaning which an oppositional culture has to understand and challenge, and indicates the importance that such work has for its constituency audience; the tension between form and content in the show itself paralleled the tension between the needs and political development of individuals in the group and the consciousness of an audience or parts thereof, engaged in sexual politics.

Monstrous Regiment then commissioned a play from David Edgar, who devised it in collaboration with Susan Todd and the company. *Teendreams*[4] toured in 1979. It was a cleverly structured picaresque political saga of 1968 and after, focusing on two women: Frances, a middle-class teacher who goes through the left in the late 1960s, through feminism in the 1970s, and into a pragmatic despair about the impossibility of changing people; and Rosie, happy wife and mother, who joins a women's group, leaves home with her children, gets divorced and starts a new life. It was a fragmentary play, uncertain about its centre; was it about feminism, or was it about all politics and idealism as illusion? At one level it certainly was an effective polemical examination of the gap between the euphoria of 1968 and the sincere but arrogant assumptions on the part of young intellectual activists that revolutionary changes in consciousness and society can happen at the flick of a switch; but the relationship of this to feminism was unclear. Feminism was seen as being as full of 'illusions' as any other political ideology, but the central dilemma which centres on Frances's relationship with two of her working-class pupils was posed and not developed. As a middle-class feminist, Frances tries to influence her students and fails. She is attacked by a male colleague and cannot vindicate herself; at one level the play is about political despair, but it also implicitly indicted the effectiveness of feminism as a force for social change.

Also in 1979, the company collectively adapted Anita Loos' *Gentlemen Prefer Blondes*, which was later rescripted by Bryony Lavery, and toured into 1980. After this the company took three months for workshops and discussions, to take stock of work and policy so far, and to plan future work.

The company's next two plays came from women writers from other countries: *Dialogue Between a Prostitute and one of her*

Clients by Italian writer Dacia Maraini (1980). The play was a two-hander, for a man and a prostitute, in which the 'fourth wall' illusion was interrupted at intervals while the cast of two involved the audience in discussion about the issues just raised. The approach to prostitution in the play itself was very much from the standpoint of a Catholic-based culture; thus there were interesting parallels made between the Italian male's fantasies about prostitution and his apparent mother-fixations. In a sense the take on prostitution was very basic indeed – a kind of first-step attempt to raise the audience's consciousness about the nature of the 'game'. It was also the first time in which the cast had engaged in direct polemical contact with the audience, and took personal responsibility for some of the ideas expressed. It was an interesting experiment for the company, but an oversimplistic theatrical event, which would have worked better in an educational/drama context.

The second play from abroad was *Mourning Pictures* by Honor Moore (1981), an American play, written in a free verse style, and about a dying mother and her daughter. The language was very different from the previous play: interior monologues in a poetic mode, and a swift-moving structure alternating between the 'real' story of the family, and the psychic realities of its members. In 1981 the company did *Yoga Class*, written for them by Rose Tremain, a young novelist. In many ways this suffered from the same kinds of problems as the Women's Theatre Group play *Soap Opera*; in its hermetic setting (a gym, to which five women and a man come for a weekly yoga class), in which the chief project seemed to be to outline the nature of yoga, and give us atomised insights into the lives of the characters. And like *Soap Opera* it was caught between the difficult tension of more than some dramatic tedium, and the first-base importance of placing the experiences of women on stage. The play also gave a chance to the performers to explore other ways of being physical onstage – all had to be physically fit and capable of doing the yoga exercises, so that audiences were confronted with, at the very least, the sight of women onstage in a physically strong alternative form to the conventionally feminine. As will be seen in a later discussion of Claire Luckham's play *Trafford Tanzi*, this was an area which was also being explored in other plays and shows.

During 1982 the company performed two plays, again in

contrasting styles: *Shakespeare's Sister*, originally written and performed by the Théâtre de l'Aquarium in Paris. The title of the play was taken from a passage in Virginia Woolf's beautiful belle-lettre on women writers, *A Room of One's Own*, in which she imagined what would have happened to a mythical Shakespeare's sister if she had tried to become a playwright. In fact, the title was about all that came from the Woolf original; for the rest the show was chiefly constructed out of a series of potent visual images exploring the ideology of conventional bourgeois marriage. Four brides scrub the floor in stylised movements, dressed in identical white; one of them shuts herself in a huge, lighted fridge. The language was a mixture of satirised clichés, some choral speaking, and cleverly choreographed movement. In ideological terms (like the *Prostitute* play) the 'message' about women and marriage was a simplistic version of the kinds of analysis which were generated at the beginning of the 1970s, but it was the translation into emotive theatrical imagery which gave it its novelty and effect.

The other play during 1982 was *The Execution*, a vast and somewhat unwieldy play by Melissa Murray, about Russian revolutionaries. It was ambitious, but lacked the clarity of focus necessary to achieve its ambitions.

The next three shows, during 1983 and 1984, were women-only shows. The group did not make any explicit announcement to that effect; they also coincided with periods during which the founder members of the company took time off to go and work elsewhere. The first production, *Fourth Wall* by Franca Rame and Dario Fo, the Italian writers, consisted of four monologues by a woman, acted by Paola Dionisotti, and with a singer, Maggie Nichols, punctuating the monologues with improvised sound. The production was in fact 'hosted' by Monstrous Regiment, rather than initiated by them, and kept the company in production, while its members took a break until much later that year. The next two shows were initiated by different members of the company. Two women performers, Gillian Hanna and Mary McCusker, were in *Calamity Jane*, by Bryony Lavery, a rather unwieldy, if affectionate, look at the life and times of the Wild West heroine. The other play was devised by company member Chris Bowler: *Enslaved by Dreams* (1984) returned to the interest in performance style which characterised *Shakespeare's Sister*, and was a demonstrative collage taken from the writings of Florence Nightingale. Fragments of her life showed the reality of her tough life, her commitment to her work, her own fight against illness, and her writing, in an imagistic and carefully textured show. Although it incorporated little direct comment on its subject matter, it was the most successful of the performance-based shows which the company attempted.

Conclusions

These three companies represent the shop-window front of the relationship between sexual politics and the theatre. Together they have foregrounded the importance of women and gay experience as subject matter for drama, and by the very nature of their group-ings, have made visible and challenged the assumptions that real and important theatre has to be seen to be dominated by the conventionally acceptable (heterosexual) white male. All their productions have in some way been marked by a sense of oppo-sition to the dominant culture, even where the work may have been hasty, unsatisfying and simplistic in what it says. In a sense one of the very important claims which they all implicitly make is the right to exist, to control their work, to take risks and to 'fail' or be uneven in quality – in other words, just like any other old theatre or company. Having said that, it is important to examine their different histories, patterns of development and methods of working, to see what questions have been raised for a theatre which, in simply seeking to represent its own sexual-political inter-ests, is inevitably seen as going out on a limb. The paradoxical positioning of all three groups is expressed through a comment from performer Mary McCusker, a founder member of Monstrous Regiment:

> Often you don't get valid criticism of the work for its own sake; your work is somehow examined as though it comes from a ghetto place, like you're coming from some strange planet.
>
> (Interview with Michelene Wandor, *Plays and Players*, June 1983)

The Women's Theatre Group is the longest-running, full-time, all-women's group. Although its present history span was really marked from the point after the Almost Free season in 1973, its real roots extend back to the earlier Women's Street Theatre Group, and there was an important ideological continuity between the two. It has remained true to the principles of collective devising, whilst also being open to the more collaborative, individual, skill-based work involving specialist writers and directors. It has also retained, in much of its work, a clear desire to present the experience of working-class women – a socialist-feminist perspective which has been greatly helped by the fact that the group excludes men. This may sound paradoxical, but it is one of the exciting paradoxes of the decision for women to develop a perspective upon the world in which they take responsibility for all its aspects. In this context it is interesting to compare the product of the all-women group with Monstrous Regiment's mixed group, which was composed out of a desire, as Mary McCusker put it, to be 'a feminist group that was non-separatist'.

The very existence of all-women groups raises the hackles of those who instinctively (though they may not always be aware of it) want to preserve the male-dominated traditions of theatre – bourgeois and socialist. Such people decry all-women groups as 'ghettoised', as 'preaching to the converted', and other kinds of boring clichés which simply close off discussion, instead of opening it up. In the case of the Women's Theatre Group, the combination of the radical feminist principle of women organising together, developing solidarity and support, with the socialist-feminist aim of representing working-class experience, has produced a range of theatrical work which does not fight shy of conflicts between women – whether of a class or a cultural nature. They have done so sometimes effectively, sometimes simplistically, but they have been able to do so because they have (for the purposes of their work) been 'free' of the risks of a mixed group in which men can either crudely or categorically be represented as the enemy (as happened in Monstrous Regiment's play *Dialogue with a Prostitute*), and where the male performers have to play the 'baddy', or in which men can be let off the hook. Throughout the first few years of Monstrous Regiment's work, it seemed to me that, with all the best intentions in the world, they had landed themselves with an obstacle to their own development, in deciding to reverse conventional power relations, and instead of men dominating the group, having women dominate the group. In 1983 Mary McCusker, one of the group's founder members, commented on their working relationships with men in the group:

> At first I found rehearsals far freer, because men were in a minority. I felt as a performer that I felt able to be more adventurous, to be able to take discussions in any direction I wanted without feeling that I was just being anecdotal or irrelevant, but it has become more complicated. For example, I think in some ways we were very protective of the men, because whenever we interviewed men we were very keen to make sure that it wasn't as bad for them in a company with more women, as it had been for us in a company which was mainly men. It also works the other way – one of the men who's worked a lot with us has said that he finds it difficult as a man saying what he thinks a predominantly female group should be doing. I began to wish that we'd gone through the stage of having only women in the company, because I feel my attitude towards women and power is very complex, and I've felt that the women expected more of each other than they ever have of the men – you want each other to be perfect, almost. Even if there's only been the one man in the group, and we've been interviewing people for the job, that male voice of authority still seems to have more weight attached to it, even if he is in the minority.
>
> (*Plays and Players, ibid.*)

The work produced by the groups, taken together with their different starting points, reveals interestingly different political trajectories. The Women's Theatre Group moved from a strong and clearly articulated political-feminist start, towards developing a stronger and more sophisticated artistic base. Monstrous Regiment, on the other hand, seem to have done the opposite, and started from a valid desire to place women's experiences centre-stage, but in assuming they could simply do so in a mixed group (albeit with men in a minority), to have dismissed the political difficulties – external and internal – which might arise. They have moved from a strong artistic base towards a stronger political base for their work. These differences, however, while important as part of a historical assessment, also indicate something of the variety of approaches which will affect the ways in which women are placed as the subject matter of drama. There is no right 'pure' way, but it does seem extremely necessary, both for the process and the product, for women to seek out the experience of working with all-women groups, and it is interesting that Monstrous Regiment seemed to have arrived at that conclusion too. Of course, both groups will continue to function and hopefully to flourish, and the future may bring very different kinds of experiences and conclusions.

Both these groups have had the blessing of regular funding over the years, and this has enabled visible continuities to develop, even though both groups have had various turnovers of personnel. Gay Sweatshop's economic security has been far more precarious. In their early years they had to submit annual applications for grants, and through the 1980s have so far worked only on one-off grants for particular projects. This has had something of a paradoxical effect. On the one hand it has made real continuity of work very hard indeed, but on the other it has meant that many of the people working on Gay Sweatshop productions have continued similar work elsewhere.

After the success of the Women's Festival, at the Drill Hall in 1977, a group calling itself the Women's Project continued a broad-based feminist and lesbian interest in a mini-season of two plays. I wrote a play called *AID Thy Neighbour*,[5] directed by Kate Crutchley at the Theatre at New End in London, which was a pastiche West End comedy about two couples, one heterosexual, one lesbian, both of whom wanted to have a baby. The play explored what was then (1978) a tabloid press 'scandal' – the practice of a tiny number of sympathetic doctors in providing artificial insemination by donor (AID) to women, both heterosexual and lesbian. The end had an ironic twist, designed to suggest that desires for parenthood, let alone the physiological ability to conceive, were not matters which anyone could really take for granted – a kind of gentle satire on the idea of the nuclear family and the principles which are assumed to underpin it. The second play was *Confinement* by Kate Phelps and Nancy Diuguid, which was produced at Oval House in London, about the experiences of a group of women in prison, and the different ways they coped with such 'confinement'. The play boasted a brilliant piece of design by Mary Moore, a circular metal construction, upon which the entire action took place. Neither of these plays was organisationally linked with Gay Sweatshop, but there was continuity in terms of some of the personnel. In 1980 the Women's Project produced *Domestic Front* by Joyce Cheeseman, at the Drill Hall, directed by Kate Crutchley, a simple, naturalistic piece about the relationships between three generations of women. The same team of writer and director worked on a dramatisation of Isabel Miller's *Patience and Sarah*, the story of the relationship between two American women in the nineteenth century. This was produced at the Oval House in 1983, where Kate Crutchley was the co-ordinator.

Looking at the differences in form and content between the men's work and the women's work in Gay Sweatshop, it is interesting to note that there have been various gender divides: the men's work has often had a greater literary and theatrical sophistication about it, perhaps in keeping with the higher theatrical profile of male homosexuals, while the women's work has often been more low-key, realistic, and concerned with the here and now. For the men historical reconstruction has been easier because of this historical visibility – the cabaret of Weimar Germany, the documentation on nineteenth-century male sexual radicals, while not exactly common knowledge, are at least somewhat more accessible than the more hidden histories of lesbianism. There is no simple conclusion to the direction which Gay Sweatshop's work will take in the future, but certainly, like the other two groups discussed, it is clear that there are still infinite possibilities for the representation of gay experience and perspectives.

Other theatrical developments

Between 1971 and 1978 Arts Council subsidy rose from around £7,000 to £1,500,000 to fringe theatre. The three groups whose work I have described in some detail may have been the most visible and they were certainly helped in this by being London-based – but throughout the second half of the 1970s there was a noticeable increase in new groups of women performers, the occasional gay play, plus younger women writers getting their work put on. 1978 marked the fiftieth anniversary of the granting of the vote to women on the same terms as to men – perhaps just one of those fortuitous coincidences – but my files, notes and collection of programmes from 1978–9 show a flourish of new and interesting work. One of the reasons, perhaps, was that it had been nearly a decade since the presence of feminism and sexual politics had begun to dent the consciousness of theatre workers, students and drama school products. New generations of young people had a far wider choice of where to put their theatrical talents and political interests than had their counterparts of an earlier decade, and with the prospect of the possibility of subsidy at some point, energies were high. The relationship between these groups and feminism was sometimes somewhat ambiguous, since many of them did not want to call themselves, or be called, 'feminist' – a mixed blessing, perhaps, since while it implied that things were now easier for women (which in certain minor respects was true), it also implied that the need for feminism was over, and that women could now have an easy time in the theatre (which was not true).

Monstrous Regiment's interest in exploring cabaret forms, which was described earlier, was in some respects linked to the work of these new groups, which put the emphasis on vigorous entertainment – women and fun. The names which these groups chose for themselves marked a departure from the more earnest, didactically oriented names of the Women's Theatre Group and even Monstrous Regiment. These groups brought a fresh and original slant to female performance, with a greater freedom towards the representation of both hetero- and homosexuality, and an exploratory approach to women's appropriation of comedy, of which they are so often the butts.

Clapperclaw formed towards the end of 1977, and although the original performing trio had not planned to be all-female, they enjoyed working together so much that it became a conscious decision. Their work was close to busking – down-market casual dress, songs, jokes, exchanges of comic banter, all with a sense of self-irony and feminist satire. Cunning Stunts, formed the same year, chose a mischievously Spoonerist title and cultivated a witty and deliberately absurdist performance style, using clowning and acrobatics, with a physical freedom onstage rare for women outside circuses. Hormone Imbalance began in early 1979, started by women who had been in Gay Sweatshop but were tired of 'agitprop come-out' plays and wanted to include comedy and self-irony in their work. Their first show was a revue written by Melissa Murray. Bloomers formed in 1978 with a first show based on working-class women's experiences, again exploring a female humour based on the revue format.

Perhaps the most successful of the semi-anarchic shows which opened avenues for a freer female comedy was the first produced by a group called Beryl and the Perils, formed in 1978. Their first show in that year was *Is Dennis Really the Menace?* directed by Michele Frankel, which was about the conditioning of women into fearful and repressed behaviour about their bodies and their sexual lives. The 'play' was a series of illustrative sketches, and the four performers took their point of departure from the Dandy/Beano comic strip characters. They wore striped and slightly wacky clothes, their faces streaked with make-up – like children who have raided the attic for clothes and their mother's dressing-table for decoration. The very end of the play had each performer making a 'personal' statement about her beliefs about sexuality – a rather lame attempt to make the ideas explicit and a personal communication between performer/audience. But despite this anti-climax, the bulk of the show was funny, powerful and totally original in feminist or gay theatre.

The chosen form gave them the physical and verbal freedom of pre-pubescent children before they have become shy and sexually self-conscious. This made the message all the more effective; as they satirised a misunderstanding in the sex life of a married couple, their own movements and gestures showed us freer and alternative ways of being, all the more effective since we knew that we were seeing adult women 'pretending' to be children. There was a meshing between form and content in which the one continually reinforced the other, together producing an impact which was immediate and complex, never reducible to a single statement from any one of the performers.

The show also implicitly questioned the audience's attitude to the female stage presence: the tension between appearance (child-like, free) and subject matter (adult, fraught) challenged the audience by (a) making it difficult (perhaps not entirely impossible) for us (men and women) to respond to them voyeuristically as glamour or 'sex objects', and (b) enabling us to see, via the innocence of the recognisable comic-strip imagery, the way that conventional 'female' ideology and upbringing can be subverted as we watch.

A different attempt to subvert the audience's voyeuristic expectations was made by a group called the Sadista Sisters, who first performed in 1974, and then reformed in 1978. They combined heavy rock music with feminist lyrics in an aggressive cabaret performance style – messily dressed, throwing food around and disembowelling a doll in a kind of adult female punk, overturning the assumption that women are neat and clean and keep the domestic world ticking over. Their style was a chaotic kind of sexual aggression which at times blotted out subtlety.

Interest in women's work was growing, and there was such a diversity around that many venues held mini-festivals: during 1978 both the Young Vic and the Battersea Arts Centre held programmes of plays, music, readings and talks, and the energy even affected the classical bastions of the Royal Shakespeare Company and the National Theatre. Julia Pascal, performer turned director, devised and directed *Men Seldom Make Passes*, a compilation of Dorothy Parker's work, as a 'platform' performance at the National Theatre in 1978. The National had not done a single play written or directed by a woman since it moved into its South Bank premises, and this platform production – ordinary dress events done as curtain-raisers to the main show – was a small step towards redressing this imbalance. Some of the actresses in the heavily male-dominated National Company had begun to discuss their conditions of work, the paucity and limited scope of the roles offered to them. Actress Maggie Ford recalled how during the autumn of 1978 there was an announcement over the tannoy that there was to be a meeting for the women, to which one of the male performers responded: 'What are you going to discuss – knitting patterns and period pains?' There was some attempt to contact women writers, but the campaign which concentrated on trying to get more and better parts for actresses didn't get very far. A rather vapid little play called *L.I.P.S.*, by one of the National's actors, was done as another Platform, affording eight parts for actresses, but the National's main repertory and employment practices were unaffected by the flurry of questioning consciousnesses.

Various other theatrical events took note of the higher profile of women in theatre; a production of Brecht's *Arturo Ui* by Rob Walker at the Half Moon Theatre in London, in 1978, used actresses to double for some of the male characters – actress Maggie Steed played 'The Barker, Butcher, Prosecutor, Woman', showing an imaginative approach to casting which could easily be applied to many more plays.

A new departure in the relationship between today's feminists and yesterday's theatre was initiated by the group Mrs Worthington's Daughters, which was initially spurred by the research which Julie Holledge was doing for her book on women in the Edwardian theatre, *Innocent Flowers*. The group began, like Monstrous Regiment, with a mixed composition, with women in the majority. Their original policy was to perform 'plays from the past either by or about women', and their first programme in early 1979 was a double bill consisting of *The Oracle* by Susanna Cibber, who, as Mrs Cibber, was a leading lady at Drury Lane Theatre in the mid-eighteenth century; and *In The Workhouse*, written in 1910 by Margaret Wynne Nevinson, a Hampstead poor law guardian. Later that year they also revived *The Twelve-Pound Look*, by J. M. Barrie, written in 1910 in support of the suffrage movement. (Earlier in 1978 Sidewalk Theatre company had toured a programme of suffragette songs, monologues and sketches called *How the Vote Was Won*.)

In the autumn of 1979 Mrs Worthington's Daughters toured with *Aurora Leigh*, which I had dramatised from the verse novel by Elizabeth Barrett Browning, published in 1857, about a woman writer's relationship to love, art and politics. It retained the iambic pentameter form, posing the group the challenge of working with verse, something not readily attempted by political companies. In 1980 the group toured *Rutherford & Son* by Githa Sowerby (first performed in 1912), the story of an Edwardian patriarch and the effect of his paternalism on his family, which I abridged for them. After this the company produced *Angels of War*, in 1981, written in 1935 by Muriel Box, writer and film-maker. This was a social-realist play which reflected the preoccupations of many women writers after the First World War with pacifism, and women in the forces. The company was only funded for specific projects, and their next productions were both in 1982; the first, *Wyre's Cross*, by Peta Masters and Geraldine Griffiths, was an ever-changing spoof feminist soap opera, performed on succeeding evenings, and put on as part of the month long festival called Women Live, in May 1982 – about which more later. Another play from the 1930s, which the company did later in 1982, was *Alison's House* by American playwright Susan Glaspell, which was loosely based on the story of poet Emily Dickinson and her family.

Finally, during this period, there was a very exciting injection of theatre work from other countries, through visiting companies and productions. First, Spiderwoman Theater, a multi-racial group based in New York, who brought over a double bill in the summer of 1978. They used minimal set and props, not just because they were a touring group, but because a maximum emphasis was thus put on the visual impact of the performers. In one of their plays, *Women in Violence*, each performer rooted her persona in a clown image, a walking picture with a jumble of character clothes, paint and gestures. Although many of the English groups had begun to explore more physical stage presences, there was a stronger physical intensity about Spiderwoman's work, which echoed the encounter and movement-based work of earlier experimental groups such as La Mama in America. Their work also drew heavily on ideas about ritual and a performance-based use of satire; a number of startling stage images rang the changes on explorations of different kinds of violence, aggression between women, a mock parody of male sexual aggression in the subway, with a strong verbal text which often demonstrated how close impulses of violence are to the psychotic violence against the self. The coherence and exuberance of the company was very different from much indigenous work.

Another, far more upmarket product, was a production of *The Club*, by American Eve Merriam. This consisted of a compilation of turn-of-the-century songs, sketches and jokes, the genuine material which was performed in American all-men clubs. The stage setting was that of an exclusive, 'classy', all-male, white club, complete with page and 'black boy'. All the material was collated 'straight'; the gloss and commentary were provided by the fact that the entire cast was female, all impeccably dressed in the requisite tie and tails. Here was a subtle use of the cross-dressing convention in which a change of form – women dressed as men – worked to subvert both the tone of the material and the expectations of the audience. What was interesting was that the material was so structured that the beginning of the show alternated anti-woman jokes with woman-as-rose songs. As the show progressed, with the performers all inhabiting the male-impersonation role, the impact of the material began to change subtly, so that it began to carry a satiric edge without the performers having to do anything other than present it in its cabaret convention. A song using a walking stick as a prop thus became a rather witty anti-phallic send-up, because of the way the actress played with subtle innuendo. The show was not a commercial success, in part because it was staged in the awkwardly shaped Regent Theatre; but it achieved a level of gentle but sophisticated subversion which has not really yet been matched. It had a British cast, which perhaps aided the impersonation of the 'gentlemanly' persona.

The other import was the work of French director – or perhaps it is more appropriate to call her a 'metteuse en scène' – Simone Benmussa. She directed English productions of some of the work she had done in Paris, which echoed some of the preoccupations of gender roles which *The Club* satirised. Benmussa's work, however, involved a delicate and entirely original kind of staging, in which she told stories about dream, psychic identification with gender, and used visual and verbal theatrical illusion (including holograms) to tease questions and meanings about gender assumptions. Two plays staged at the Theatre at New End introduced her to English audiences: *The Singular Life of Albert Nobbs* was based on a short story by George Moore, in which a young woman disguises herself, and lives out her life as a man, in order to be securely employed as a waiter. The story is simple and moving; the choice to live disguised as a man has condemned Nobbs to loneliness and monasticism. When she begins to imagine a life with companionship, she also encounters disappointment and pain. The play was staged with 'stars' – Susanna York and Julia Foster; and Benmussa managed to suggest both the possibility of more fluid gender roles and the pain of too rigid a gender definition at the same time, as well as indicating through her use of movement the subtleties of real life and dream life. The same intellectual and perceptual delicacy marked her other work, *Portrait of Dora*, by Helene Cixous, about one of Freud's women patients (1979), *The Revolt* by Villiers de l'Isle Adam (1980), and *Appearances* (1980), credited to Benmussa 'after Henry James'.

Agitational theatre continued into the late 1970s through the work of groups like Broadside Mobile Workers Theatre, a mixed socialist group, who developed a play on the Working Women's Charter which they performed, with modifications, between 1975 and 1980; Counteract (also mixed) have done agitprop plays on women's work, and rape; and in 1979 a new group calling themselves Spare Tyre formed to devise a play called *Baring the Weight*, based on the book *Fat is a Feminist Issue* by Susie Orbach, which analysed women's attitudes to weight and their bodies. The members of the groups had all had weight problems of different kinds and the discussions after the play were designed to encourage women in the audience to develop a more positive attitude, as group members felt they had.

Across the spectrum of sexual politics in the alternative theatre the 1970s saw an interesting development: the vivid visual imagery of the early street theatre, with its spontaneity and its attack on stereotypical 'feminine' imagery gave way in the mid-1970s to a period of consolidation and the development of a theatre of argument, a theatre which explored what it would mean to reclaim the experience of women and gays from the militant sexual-political perspective of the period. Such a reclamation entailed reversing the conventional priorities of male heterosexual experience, and also altering its class perspective (more overtly in the work of feminist and lesbian theatre). The third phase, towards the end of the 1970s, showed a return to some of the early spontaneity, but now in a different context; instead of using dressing-up and visual imagery to challenge the audience's assumptions about real-life oppression, the new spontaneity revolved round an examination of the way the theatrical forms themselves work to represent sexuality. This development came about not simply as a result of an abstract or theoretical decision that this was the 'correct' thing to do, but from the confidence and freedom which many women performers developed as a result of that early, simple, agitational work. The new work subverted existing entertainment forms and by so doing began to open up the possibility of an original female performance style: showing how women can annihilate the feminine options in theatre. In any case, the processes of reclamation, reversal and subversion often overlap.

The fierce (sometimes puritanical) anti-authoritarianism of the early 1970s 'collective' approach to theatre work attacked the oppressive mystiques attached to the social division of labour. The work of feminist and gay groups took up this 'collective' approach, by asserting the needs of feminist and gay performers to control their own work. As the work established itself, the re-establishment of respect for individual skills led the groups to employ designers, directors and writers, and this process also gave workers with non-performing skills a chance to develop their own sexual-political attitudes. Thus the dissemination of a feminist and gay consciousness from the base lines of the 'specialist' groups discussed in these chapters is crucial.

Organisation

In October 1978, The Feminist Theatre Study Group organised a week of action, picketing five West End shows and handing out leaflets to draw attention to the situation of actresses and the content of the plays:

> Did the characters in this play imply that:
> – Blondes are dumb?
> – Wives nag?
> – Feminists are frustrated?
> – Whores have hearts of gold?
> – Mothers-in-law interfere?
> – Lesbians are aggressive?
> – Intellectual women are frigid?
> – Women who enjoy sex are nymphomaniacs?
> – Older women are sexless?
> We are a group of theatre workers who are tired of portraying these cardboard cut-outs.
> We want theatre managers, directors and writers to stop producing plays which insult women.

The group ceased meeting during 1979, but some of the women initiated a series of conferences under the banner of 'Women in

Entertainment'. During the course of 1980 various subgroups continued to meet – groups discussing 'Women and Humour', 'Women Directors and Administrators', and a Women Writers group. The most visible and vigorous of these was the Women Directors and Administrators group, and, with the help of Jo Caust and Susan Feldman, students at the City University arts administration course, a large conference was organised in March 1980. Out of this sufficient energy was generated for the organisation to give itself a more formal and grand title: the Standing Conference of Women Theatre Directors and Administrators. It is not surprising, given the organisational and managerial functions which go with the jobs of directing and administration, that this grouping of women should have initiated a number of small discussion meetings, and two more large conferences. The first of these was held later in 1980, called 'Women and Creativity', with guest speaker Kate Millett. The second major conference, held at the end of 1982, was on the broad subject of 'Women Writers Talking – Is There a Women's Culture', and did not confine itself to discussion about theatre. As director Sue Dunderdale pointed out, the group was in danger of diffusing its energies, and needed to return its attention to the particular needs of theatre. The conference's objectives were then more clearly defined:

> (a) Conference is committed to achieving equal rights and opportunities for women theatre directors and administrators and will adopt a radical campaigning policy to achieve these aims.
> (b) Conference will act as a pressure group in pursuance of the acceptance of feminist perspectives in the profession, whilst creating more job opportunities and a better working climate for women in all areas of theatre.
> (c) Conference will provide a forum for the definition of these perspectives and develop a debate on the inherent values of our work as women, through a constant exchange of ideas and experience.
>
> (Conference Papers, 1979–81)

At the beginning of 1983, the conference commissioned a survey about the employment of women directors, administrators and playwrights. Sue Dunderdale's account of the survey is worth quoting because it presents a clear digest of the findings and the conclusions:[6]

> There are three main areas of focus in the survey, those of director, administrator, and playwright. This is because a theatre's programme and employment policy will generally be decided by the director, often in consultation with the administrator. The playwright will produce the cultural matter and messages and will have a strong influence on employment and will determine the dominant gender amongst the actors employed. It is necessary to note here that Equity quote 14 weeks per year in work as the average for their male members, and seven weeks per year for their female members.
>
> The survey was conducted by telephone, for speed and efficiency, during April/May 1983. It focused on producing theatres throughout England and Wales. Scotland was not included because we couldn't afford it. Only two theatres refused to co-operate by phone. The period investigated was September 1982–September 1983. This period was chosen specifically to avoid artificial inflation of figures produced by the 'Women Live Festival' in May 1982. We contacted:
> 52 out of 54 Repertory Theatres
> 24 out of 26 Fringe Theatres
> 41 out of 61 Alternative/Community Theatre Companies.
>
> The theatres we excluded were: amateur; co-operatives; drama schools; children's theatres and companies; youth and Theatre in Education companies; seasonal summer theatres; touring venues and commercial companies. Children's theatres and any educationally based theatres have been excluded because they are traditionally areas of female occupation, also the focus of the survey is mainstream theatre culture. We also excluded commercial companies because they do not generally produce cultural initiatives and are, in the main, privately funded. All the theatres and companies concerned in the survey are publicly funded. This may be seen by many as a public endorsement of the values and assumptions laying at the base of these institutions. When you examine the findings of the survey you should remind

yourself of the contribution in taxes and rates made by women towards the funding of the arts and also remember that women are the majority of arts graduates and theatre audiences.

It will probably by now be no surprise to you to learn that the survey confirms our subjective experience and conforms with the general picture of lack of female representation in other decision making areas of society. The theatre world proves itself to be no more progressive than any of the other professions. In the poorest, least well subsidised areas of theatre, alternative and community, we find our largest congregation of women. Many of these women will have chosen to work in alternative theatre, they did not however choose to work for poor wages and with unworkably low budgets. Women are not well represented in the more established Fringe theatres, whose radical origins do not seem to have generated a radical practice. In the reps we find a small minority of women resident artistic directors and even fewer resident administrators; however important the roles, we do not cover in the survey publicity officers or secretarial and box office staff, many of whom are women. The two major national subsidised companies have no female resident artistic or associate directors and no female top administrators. The RSC produced some figures for freelance directors but these referred to women used, either for no or very little payment, to direct for the 1983 Barbican Festival. A microcosm of the general experience of women being asked to perform the most menial tasks in any particular power structure.

If . . . you examine the condensed list of results of the survey, it must become clear to you that the more money and more prestige a theatre has, the less women will be employed in decision making positions and the less women will be on the board. Hence women are the least subsidised artists in the theatre and have least influence in determining policy and programme. Now that we have the survey, it is up to us, the Standing Conference, to use it in a campaign to put an end to the pro-male discrimination that we find is so prevalent. However, we also hope that you will use these new or reawakened perceptions to influence and change the present appalling situation. We must begin to find out who is on our theatre boards and campaign for equal male/female representation. We must seek out and support the women who are managing to find work; and we must start to pressure those who award subsidy to make demands about access to and control over that subsidy by women. It is up to us to ensure that the situation revealed by the survey is not allowed to continue.[7]

In a leaflet publicising its 1985 AGM, the conference listed a concrete programme of action:

Funding Bodies
Equal opportunity policies, including no discrimination against women, should be a condition of public subsidy for theatres.
Individuals Working in the Theatre
Commitment for all theatre workers to break down attitudinal barriers and to establish equal access to employment for women.
Theatres
All theatres should apply an active equal opportunities policy and monitor its operation. Theatres' staffing committees, advisory bodies and boards of directors should reflect the breadth of society that the theatre serves and have a healthy male/female balance.

Alongside the work which the Standing Conference was pursuing, Women in Entertainment continued organising. Its original intentions were to broaden the basis of women organising to include all the entertainment industries – a laudable if somewhat unattainable aim, given their meagre resources. The energies of the initiating women turned in 1980 to organising 'Women Live', 'a month of nationwide activity with an emphasis on women throughout the entertainment industry'. The date fixed for this was May 1982, to give the optimum time for women to organise all over the country, in whatever medium. In 1981 Women in Entertainment produced a 'Writers' Directory', which included women writing for stage, screen and radio. They produced regular newsletters and bulletins, and the energy generated, together with regional organising by women on the spot, did produce a wide range of work all over the country, including films, exhibitions, theatre, music, poetry, dance, discussions. The month was a curious mixture of shop window action and real achievement. Some publicity was gained, drawing attention both to the varied and valuable work women were doing in the arts, and to the areas in which they were poorly represented. But it was noticeable that in London, where the volume of theatre work by women had in any case increased immensely compared with five years before, the events during May 1982 did not seem to be significantly increased. Outside London, however, the focus for that month provided support for women to find and create opportunities for work which otherwise might have been difficult. It meant that touring theatre groups were part of a whole series of events, instead of being just the one token 'women's event', and it meant that newspapers and the radio gave more attention than usual to what women were doing. However, there were in some theatres some rather cynical attitudes: theatres who had only commissioned one woman writer that year made sure her play was scheduled for May 1982 to ensure the maximum exposure for the theatre, without the theatre policy itself altering. As Julia Pascal pointed out:

> *Women Live* is a shout against this concealment of women's work, and, while it has to be supported for the month of May 1982, it is very obvious that in June 1982, the traditional power structures which include women, will be very much alive . . . *Women Live* in May 1982 certainly. But women are alive and kicking for fifty-two weeks of the year. So the Boys in Charge had better look out.
>
> (*The Literary Review*, May 1982)

6

The skilled process

Performers

The alternative theatre companies have been largely performer-managed; a feature which highlights the fact that in traditional theatre work the performer is the least powerful in the creative process. Since the demise of the actor/manager (or the occasional actress/manageress) the performer has generally come to be seen as an interpreter of the text's and/or director's intentions. As part of the post-Second World War changes in the theatre industry, the 'image' of the performer changed too. The star system, still very much in evidence throughout the West End theatre of the 1950s, was undergoing modification. A shift in the class content of post-war drama affected the image of the male actor:

> Within ten years suave actors had been replaced by rough
> ones as heroes, metropolitan accents by regional ones,
> complacent young men by angry ones, stylish decadents by
> frustrated 'working-class' anti-heroes.
> (John Elsom, *Post-War British Theatre*, Routledge & Kegan
> Paul, 1979, p. 34)

Elsom concentrates exclusively on the image of the actor – but gradually changes in the family and the position of women also began to affect the image of the actress. Sheila Allen, who left the Royal Academy of Dramatic Art in 1951, commented:

> The current heroine at that time was five foot, four inches;
> a sort of fluffy little blonde, light, effervescent. I was five

foot seven and a half inches, and I was told at drama school that I would have problems because I was very tall. By the mid-sixties that had changed – with leading ladies like Vanessa Redgrave and Glenda Jackson, now you could be a heroine and it didn't matter so much what you looked like.

Implicit in the 'collective' experimentation described in the earlier chapters is a challenge to the conventional powerlessness of the performer; now that they could control the context and content of their work, the experience of living the feminist slogan that 'the personal is political' resulted in an intense sense that all the alienation of everyday life had been overcome. For many theatre workers this intensity was enhanced by the enthusiasm of audiences who felt they could identify with situations in a play for the first time. Such intensity tended to absorb energy. Nancy Diuguid, one of the members of Gay Sweatshop who toured with *Any Woman Can*, commented:

> The discussions afterwards were a form of political education, for the company members as well as the audience. It was terribly exciting, and we'd stay up for hours talking with people after the show. But by the end we were tired of being twenty-four-hours-a-day political lesbians; we were saying 'I need just a little personal time to myself'.

For women performers in the socialist groups in the early 1970s, bringing feminism to their work exposed a whole new aspect of power relations within the group, and tensions which had never been discussed before became explicit. Women were worried that their energy and ideas would simply be taken over by the men. Eileen Murphy, one of the Theatre-in-Education team who devised *Sweetie Pie*, tells how, when the suggestion was first made to do a Theatre-in-Education play based on the four demands of the Women's Liberation Movement:

> I was an active member of the women's movement, and although I was aware of the propagandist value of such a programme, I felt we shouldn't do it. Far from being committed to the movement, there was a great deal of unquestioned chauvinism in the group; our motives in choosing the subject at this stage were tainted by the

spurious topicality created by the condescending press coverage, and I resented the fact that hard work done by small women's groups should provide easy material for a theatre group riddled with chauvinism.

(Bolton Octagon Theatre-in-Education, *Sweetie-Pie*, Eyre Methuen, 1975, p. 15)

The early groups challenged by feminism saw it simply as 'the woman question', as a problem or issue that affected only women, and did not involve either class perspectives or male attitudes and behaviour. Red Ladder, one of the first mixed socialist groups to recognise the importance of feminism, found themselves reappraising the group's working relations when they were evolving their 'women's play', *Strike While the Iron is Hot*. One of their members, Glen Park, remembered the process they went through during the summer of 1973:

We had a phrase called WIMTWIRL, which meant 'What It Means To Work In Red Ladder', and it was to do with all the pressures that people experienced personally in their life away from the group and inside the group. To do with wanting your individual needs to be met, but because it's a collective you constantly feel you ought to repress your own needs and that creates tension. Some people do manage to get their own way, and that introduces a kind of competitive element. We started discussions about the women's play out of that dynamic, talking about our own personal histories as men and women, and for the first time making conscious the ways in which male oppression took place within the group. Everyone was very shaken up by that.

Another group member, Steve Trafford, observed: 'It was certainly true that till then the men, and the most articulate men, were dominant in the way the plays were written.' And another, Chris Rawlence, remarked on the advantages which resulted from this painful process:

For the first time there was a kind of meeting point of people's 'personal experience' and the sort of labour movement politics that we'd been into previously. It wasn't so much 'on behalf of'; it had much more of ourselves in it.

The spread of gay activism produced similar challenges to socialist groups in the content of their work. Brian Hibberd, a performer who worked with the Bradford group, The General Will, commented on a play they did during 1970–1:

> We were doing a play on the second year of the Tory government. I don't think there was any consciousness of sexual politics at that time. There was actually a sketch in the play where Heath was being taught French by a very camp French master – the implication being that Heath was gay and the audience could have a good laugh at it. It wasn't till someone who was active in gay politics objected that we realised what we were doing.

Bradford was an important centre for feminist and gay activists, and there was some pressure from within General Will as well as outside it for it to become all-gay and serve the gay community. There were confrontations between the Gay Liberation Front and the socialists in General Will, and finally the heterosexual members left the group, which was run for a while by gay men.[1]

Some of the former members of General Will then formed a new group called Roadgang, based in Newcastle. Because activism around women's issues was growing in the area, some company members felt that those issues urgently demanded plays about them. Gradually the men left Roadgang, and one of the remaining women members commented later:

> A lot of people think that we took over the company, but in fact the men left and it wasn't so much a takeover as a leftover. At that point I don't think we realised the enormity of what we'd done, but we found that becoming a women's group, which we hadn't done at all consciously, solved the problem of our function. Before we had always had exciting, aggressive, constructive/destructive arguments about women's issues. But as an all-female group, we found that we didn't have to justify doing work on campaigns and issues specific to women.

They kept the name Roadgang for a year (1976–7) and then decided to change it, in accord with their new emphasis:

> How the name came about was sort of like a joke to start with. After the holidays someone said why don't we call ourselves Major Diversion, because although within Equity there is a left, it is still a very male-dominated left and they think the Women's movement is a major diversion from any sort of politics – just a middle-class wank. Then we came up with the other rationale that 'Major Diversion' could refer to entertainment as being a major diversion from work.

Christine Peacock, another member of the company, amplified the point which applies also to the names of many other sexual-political groups:

> It's like using the terminology which has been dominated by the male left and taking on one of their own terms and saying 'It is not your term any more'. It's like we needed to shed a skin like a snake and find a new personality.

Monstrous Regiment's decision to be a female-dominated group was slightly more conscious, although spurred largely in reaction to the male dominance of their previous individual experiences.

> There had been areas of dissatisfaction for me as an actress – I suppose to do with the treatment of women, although I couldn't have articulated it as such at that point. We'd have company meetings and I'd say what I thought about comments like 'tarts wearing PVC skirts', and trying to bring up things like that with so few women in the company was very difficult. You start feeling 'Oh, God, I'm holding everything up'.
>
> (Mary McCusker)

> I had been belly-aching for ages about women's role in the alternative theatre being similar to their role in straight theatre. I had gone to women's movement conferences, but that was all quite apart from my work in the theatre.
>
> (Gillian Hanna)

By contrast the experience of the women who formed the Women's

Theatre Group in 1974 after the Almost Free season was much closer to the Women's Liberation Movement, and their decision to be all-female was consciously rationalised:

> We did have a strong feminist policy not to have men in the group. People kept asking us how we managed without men – weren't we theatrically limited – which seemed so silly at the time. There was so much to be done. We preferred working without men.
>
> (Mica Nava)

> I'd had experiences before, when I'd been in mixed groups, where I'd feel prevented from working, either by having sexual relationships with men that were so involving that I lost my ability to concentrate on work; or being the only woman in a group of men, which was misery, being the lone voice.
>
> (Anne Engel)

> We felt that if we had men, they'd just be token men in the same way that you get one or two women in an all-male company. We'd be telling them what to do and how to behave – maybe using them in a token way to play 'baddies', because we were a strong feminist group and had criticisms of how men behave.
>
> (Lyn Ashley)

But however much the degree of control over their work was liberated by being in all-female or female-dominated groups, one problem common to the production of all touring theatre was insoluble. When the Women's Theatre Group went full time with the aid of an Arts Council grant in 1976, two of the women with children had to decide to leave. Even with the priorities of a feminist group towards linking oppression at home and at work, certain conventional attitudes and material limitations remained:

> In the end I couldn't commit myself to touring. Sometimes we did as many as three shows a day. There was a lot of conflict within the group about this. I remember I was teaching part-time in Birmingham, and this was accepted as 'real work' by the group, and they were prepared to pay

extra on my fare to get from Birmingham to Aberdeen (or
wherever we were performing), but not if I said I must have
one day this weekend for me and the kids and my family.
I felt very bitter about this, not because it was anybody's
fault, but because it was one of the realities of being in a
touring group.

(Mica Nava)

Touring is impossible with children. It wasn't just being
terribly tired, it was a strain, tearing me different ways. People
think it's like having a dog, you can dump it, or you can go
home and just feed it. But it's not, it's the time you want
to spend with them, and that they want to spend with you.

(Lyn Ashley)

The decision within Gay Sweatshop by the women to split into
an artistically autonomous group also stemmed from the reproduction of traditional male/female roles within the original group:

The men were always much more into us working together.
They were very happy to have women in the company – I
think that was partly because of using women to find out
about their own sexism – I don't put them down for that.
I also felt I couldn't work with men – a kind of emotional
reaction after I'd stage-managed a show for them on tour
and I was fulfilling the role of mother and confidante so
often, I didn't want to do it again. But I also feel we have
different issues to deal with. The fact that many gay men's
political lives revolve round the way they see each other as
sexual objects is something that is very different for us.
Lesbians have to see their oppression as part of the
oppression of women, and gay men have to confront their
own sexism and find out about it.

(Jill Posener)

The close identification which alternative theatre workers have
with their product meant that the reasons for deciding to write
any given play came from a mixture of personal/political/aesthetic
sources, but always from the desire to make an honest statement
which would communicate intimately to the audience. Jill Posener
described how she came to write *Any Woman Can*:

The men were saying they could write women's plays and I was saying they shouldn't. I didn't know why politically, but instinctively I felt that men shouldn't write for women. I wouldn't dream of writing for gay men. I'd come out as a lesbian but I played the gay clown and I was working in fringe theatre. I wrote *Any Woman Can* not because I'm a theatre writer (which I'm not) but because it was the only way I could make a statement about my sexuality, my life. If I'd have been a painter, I'd have painted it.

The debate about how close the identification between worker and product needs to be began almost inadvertently, during the first Gay Sweatshop season in 1975. Drew Griffiths, writer, director and actor, commented on the problems that casting for gay plays threw up – at that point the group had not yet decided that all performers must be gay:

We said we'd like the directors and writers to be gay, but as far as actors went, we were just employing them to do a job. In one play we had a straight actor, who was married with a child. After the first day's rehearsal I got a phone call from him and he said 'Sorry, I just can't do it'. He couldn't do a scene with another man in bed, having to relate to another man onstage in front of an audience. The disheartening thing was the gay actors we interviewed. Some of them said, 'No, no way. I can play a screaming faggot or a fairy, but I've looked at the script, it's real, this person is real. I can't do that.' What they meant was 'I can't expose myself onstage in that way. Yes, I am homosexual and people in the theatre know but there's no point in shouting it from the rooftops.'

(Drew Griffiths)

The first cast of *Any Woman Can* was similarly a mixture of heterosexual and lesbian actresses, which revealed some of the problems for heterosexual actresses in representing a positive view of lesbian experience. When the experience being presented onstage is new to the audience and to performers, there are bound to be difficulties in finding an experience on which the performer can draw for her role. The responsibility which polemical theatre has to its audience also adds pressure:

> I genuinely believe that heterosexual women cannot play lesbians convincingly. And also, if you're going to do anything that's to do with sexual politics, you've got to be able to justify it to the audience, because we're not simply in the theatre business, we're in the business of sexual politics in theatre. I realised that if afterwards the actresses couldn't totally support what they had said in the play, then it was a mistake. But I do think lesbian actresses can play heterosexuals because most of us have been heterosexual and know what it's about.
>
> (Jill Posener)

> We knew it was going to be difficult because it inevitably meant limiting your choices. They have got to be good actors, and they have got to be gay and not only do they have to be gay, they have to be politicised gay.
>
> (Drew Griffiths)

This preoccupation with expanding the democratic process was very much the hallmark of a lot of alternative theatre work in the first part of the 1970s. Over time, many groups have continued to put collaborative principles first, and, what is just as important, the hundreds of performers who at one time or another have worked in touring companies, Theatre-in-Education groups – any kind of context where they have been involved in decision-making and determining the form of their own work – have carried with them an increasing confidence when they have gone to work either in the more established theatres, or in the media of television, film, etc. Performers nurtured on the political theatre of the 1970s are far more aware of the way power works in the theatre, and have been more able to understand the way they are seen as women, to analyse it and to cope with it in different ways. Actress Harriet Walter joined 7:84, the socialist touring company, and found there – as did the performers in Red Ladder – that the gender composition of the company affected the way discussions and involvement went:

> In the 7:84 company I realised it was much easier to interrupt

a woman than a man. The sheer energy and force behind
the voice would make you hold back until there was a good
moment to speak.

(*Calling the Shots*, ed. Susan Todd, Faber, 1984, p. 19)

Since working with them, Harriet Walter's work has taken her
into successful plays on television, and with more established
theatre companies, including work with the Royal Shakespeare
Company. She recognises that male performers share certain
vulnerabilities:

> All actors are in a way the female in the relationship; they
> have to wait to be asked, invited, keep all they've got inside
> them until it's required.
>
> (*Ibid.*, p. 23)

> But once chosen, different demands are made: I get fed up
> that not so much is required of actresses as of actors. . . . Men
> quite often grow and their talents leap because the part
> requires it of them. . . . Certain questions arise about your
> work as an actress that I don't think puzzle critics about a
> male character, questions about being liked or not being
> liked, sympathetic or unsympathetic. Nobody sits there and
> says, 'Do I like Hamlet?', but in *All's Well That Ends Well*
> there are great outcries in the critical world about whether
> Helena is likeable or not.
>
> (*Ibid.*, p. 14)

And a passing comment on some of the fraught professional
conflicts which can happen between actors and actresses:

> There's an assumption in men, an arrogance that comes from
> the way the whole set-up feeds them, that their part is what
> matters most. As long as you serve their part, as an actress,
> then you're the best person they've ever worked with,
> because you're malleable. The play is assumed to be about
> him, not about this society, or all these people together, but
> about him. Lots don't do that, but lots do.
>
> (*Ibid.*, p. 19)

Actress Maggie Steed's comments on her own drama school

training showed how the attitudes which Sheila Allen described still prevailed in the early 1960s:

> I left at the age of 19, five foot nine, taller than most of the male students, with gappy teeth and the encouraging words from my principal that I was 'very talented but mustn't expect to work until I was thirty'.
>
> (*Ibid.*, p. 63)

Not finding much success through auditioning, she worked as a secretary into the early 1970s. Then, affected by the climate of cultural and political change, she returned to the theatre and worked in Theatre-in-Education in Coventry, and later with another socialist touring group, Belt and Braces. Here she was at the age of 30, in Brecht's play *The Mother*:

> My first big present. Shit, my principal was right. A number of us, women, that is, realised that we seemed to be playing a lot of men. . . . We had become quite good at playing men; we'd had a lot of practice. . . . We realised it was because the shows we were in were political shows, dealing with the capitalist world, the public world. And who runs it, this world? You've got it. A *lot* of men's parts. . . . If there were stereotypes working in Belt and Braces there are hundreds of them out there, in plays and films, art and sit-com. And even where the stereotypes don't exist in the material because of good writing, careless or cynical directing will expect them.
>
> (*Ibid.*, pp. 65–6)

Although very many classical plays contain important and rewarding parts for actresses, it is also possible to see them in a different light, and one which recognises the male-gendered perspective of most plays:

> One of the loneliest jobs I ever did was to play Gertrude in *Hamlet*. I was miserable and frustrated, and then realised that I was playing this part in this play, and all the other characters were ignoring her! She's only the lad's mother, for god's sake! It is very difficult to paint a character's life on a stage if the writer hasn't written even a few clues, and

it is also a problem because the temptation is to overpaint, bring your own frustration on to the stage with you and unbalance the play.

(*Ibid.*, p. 71)

As well as doing some very successful work on television, Maggie Steed became involved with a group of fringe performers who were instrumental in setting up 'alternative' comedy and cabaret. This really took off in 1979, at a variety of venues: at a late-night club in Soho, and very soon as part of pub-theatre, a new style of variety entertainment in pubs all over London, in which stand-up comedy rubbed shoulders with poetry, bands, sketches, all with a desire to produce comedy, jokes, satire which came from within the experiences of alternative performers (who wrote their own material) who played to young, predominantly student, audiences of a radical inclination. Part of the broadly shared aim of a very varied lot of comics was to avoid the standard fare of racist and sexist jokes which were the stock in trade of 'popular' comedy, from the northern working-men's clubs, to the glitter of television comedy.

The stand-up comedienne is a relative (though not a total) rarity. There are some women comics who take their turn in the working-men's club circuits, one of whom, veteran Olga James, described the toughness of the audiences: 'You're fighting ten pints of beer in every man, it's a battle of wits and 90 per cent of them are unarmed.' (*Guardian*, 20 December 1978.)

In her act she includes material aimed at the women in the audiences – jokes which are female equivalents to the jokes men tell about women's sexuality: 'You don't believe me, do you, girls, you can see I'm innocent, I wouldn't molest a fly . . . unless it was open.' (*Ibid.*)

Some successful women comics on television have broken somewhat new ground in bringing taboo areas of women's lives into the subject matter of their comic routines – of these, perhaps Victoria Wood is the best known, with her poignant and witty jokes about obesity, food, sex, fashion, and glamour – a confident send-up of vulnerable femininity which includes making fun of men.

The small number of women involved in the alternative cabaret came to it with a more sophisticated understanding of what they were exploring, but even here they found gender differences in the way audiences responded to their material:

> If you come on looking glamorous, showing your shoulders, you realise that the women you're trying to win don't like you because they've come with their blokes and they can see their blokes looking at you. So you throw that away and put on something less seductive and say how you've said goodbye to romance, you don't need fantasy any more and the bloke up the back shouts, 'Well, you never needed it anyway'. So you're always trying to figure how to look and how to pitch yourself. This is a problem women have that men don't.
>
> (Maggie Steed, Platform 2, Summer 1980)

The breaking of taboos is something for which the women in the audiences are very grateful; it is bound to be a risky process, however, for both performer and audience:

> I do a sketch about contraception in which I use a diaphragm. Where it goes down best and I feel happiest with it is in a mixed audience, but where the majority of women are really on my side and are overjoyed at seeing diaphragms being waved in front of their eyes, and especially in front of the men they've come with. Basically that is a mixed lefty audience.
>
> (Ibid.)

What is taboo-breaking for women may well be shocking and discomfiting for the men; for some younger male performers a solution has been to construct entertainment which, among other things, ridicules some of the excesses of masculinity to which men are subjected – comedian Simon Fanshawe, and a group called The Joeys have had notable successes in this area.

Women performers have a different relationship to their stage persona and their material, from the men. Pauline Melville, who also had extensive theatre experience on the fringe and in 'art' theatres before developing her own act, evolved a character called Edie in 1978:

Whenever I've done acting workshops, the men could always do the clowning straight away and we women were never particularly good. So I was able to develop Edie bit by bit, originally in a show which was all-women. She was successful straight away, incredibly popular, and I was asked to do her at benefits, fringe cabarets.

(Pauline Melville, in interview with the author, 1983)

Edie was a slight lady, wearing a dull peacock-green coat and hat, who stood very still behind the microphone, chatting in a very low-key way to the audience about her life, her marriage, her neighbours, and the various fads and crazes she got involved with.

Pauline Melville pinpointed another difference between the kind of comedy she felt comfortable with, and the kinds of personae developed by the men:

At one time I was under some pressure from the men to try and do something not in character – to stand up as 'me'. It is a very typical female tradition that the women will do stand-up comedy within a female character, like Joyce Grenfell, and that they won't just get up and tell a joke. For some of men, who were involved in the Lenny Bruce tradition, the really amazing thing was to be free to be yourself onstage, and I think they saw what I was doing as perhaps hiding behind a comic creation. There was enough truth in what they said to make me want to explore it more.

So I come on and do material as Pauline Melville, about my own life, my childhood, my feelings about the Queen, but whereas Edie works well most of the time, doing the material as myself works well less often. I'm not totally certain why that is. I think if you're going to do conventional stand-up comedy, you have to have a persona – that's not the same thing as a character, but some sort of strong individual identity, and perhaps that's where women find it difficult because they're so used to appearing in whatever light someone would like them to, that when they're asked to present themselves consistently and solidly in some way, they find it very difficult.

(*Ibid.*)

In the various areas of stand-up comedy, sketches – any sort of theatrical entertainment form where the relationship between the performer and audience is very direct, and where the laughter feedback is essential for the act to keep up its pace – in other words, theatre forms where the fourth wall was never there in the first place, women have both great disadvantages and enormous privileges. The disadvantage of having a fragmented tradition is perhaps one reason why women have so far been slower than men in the field, but that very disadvantage gives women the edge in terms of the excitement and power in the taboo-breaking involved in doing comedy about themselves (and experiences common to other women) and taking on the audience in the heady power relationship involved. The exhilarating novelty is that women are in charge of their own material about themselves – whether it is in 'character' or not, and to be able to tell sexual jokes, against men or against themselves, springs from a confidence that goes beyond demonstrating that women can be good sports and laugh at themselves; it also demonstrates the power women have to choose how to place themselves in comedy, slapstick or satire, and to shift the vantage point of women from largely being the butt of men's humour, to reclaiming themselves as the subject of their own.

Directors

The new opportunities for work in alternative theatre for people with non-performing skills have been particularly important for women. And contact with sexual political theatre has enabled many women to view their own work more critically. The overall division of labour in theatre which gives greater credit and status to the 'creative' than to the mere 'technical' has another dimension in the way some jobs are considered the prerogative of men, others of women. The interaction between the way the social and sexual division of labour operates provides insights into the prejudices which stand in the way of a fuller participation in theatre by women, especially where matters of power and authority are at stake.

The role of director combines many qualities which are associated with both masculinity and femininity: the director (even in alternative theatre) liaises between all the different elements during the rehearsal process, and is ultimately responsible for the artistic coherence (or 'vision', as it is sometimes called) of the production itself. In recent theatrical history the director's role has been crucial to the development of avant-garde theatre – despite the myths about the 1950s to 1960s being a period of 'writers' theatre'; in fact the initiation of new work methods, expanding the subject matter of plays and encouraging new writing resulted from directors' initiatives at theatres such as the Royal Court and the Theatre Royal, Stratford, in London. Directors who have secure jobs as directors have a great deal of power.

Although the methods of work in alternative theatre are far more open and democratic, it is inevitable that the director will hold more reins within the production process itself than anyone else. At the same time the director is traditionally supposed to have sensitivity – both towards the text and the talents of the company, and towards the personnel – keeping everyone happy. Reputations of traditional theatre directors veer from the extremes of the brilliant martinet to the sensitive coaxer, but elements of both co-exist in any director. Perhaps this combination of authority and sensitivity explains why certain kinds of gay men have been drawn towards directing: men who are known to be gay in the theatre, but who conceal the fact from the world.

The traditional notion of the male artist allows him to combine the two extremes of 'hard' and 'soft' qualities, but it has been less easy for women to do so, since female artistic authority is rarely seen in public. Although there have been some notable exceptions (for instance, Joan Littlewood), outstanding women directors have rarely stayed the course. Clare Venables outlines some of the ways in which the traditional social role of the director, combined with assumptions about women, produce particular difficulties for women directors:

> One of the problems about learning to direct . . . is that most directors don't know how other directors work. It is a very private activity carried on only in front of the actors, whom directors mystify for a good deal of the time. But firstly we know that directors, on the whole, lead rehearsals. Secondly,

that they reveal to the actors, or help the actors to discover the text. Sometimes they will tell people where to stand, where to move, sometimes they won't. They conduct operations. Beyond these facts how each director arrives at a particular result is more or less a mystery. But even these basic jobs are foreign to women's conditioning. On the whole, most of us have been taught from an early age that to 'boss people about' is not a good idea. 'A man is dynamic, a woman is bossy', and so on. So as soon as women start directing, they are initiating ideas which cut at what they have been conditioned to feel, however violently they reject that conditioning. So women have to fight the stress not only of the job itself, but their own struggle with their training.
(Conference Papers 1979–81, Standing Conference of
Women Theatre Directors and Administrators, 1981)

Theatre boards will rarely admit publicly to prejudice against employing women as directors, but the experiences of younger women point to a strong resistance. In March 1978, Julia Pascal, the first woman to direct at the National Theatre on the South Bank, compiled and directed an early evening 'Platform' performance based on the writing of Dorothy Parker. She commented on the upper male echelon at the time: 'Although they say they have no prejudice against women directors, there is very strong, perhaps unconscious prejudice.' It was not until late in 1981 that the National Theatre employed a woman as a freelance director for a major production – Nancy Meckler, who directed Edward Albee's play *Who's Afraid of Virginia Woolf*. The Royal Shakespeare Company had no woman director on its staff since Buzz Goodbody in the early 1970s – in 1981 they had two women assistant directors. When challenged, these theatres (and, to be fair, many others) answer that it is always the best person who gets the job. Such an answer inevitably defends a status quo which refuses to question the reasons for male dominance in the theatre.

Sometimes women directors themselves start by assuming that their gender is irrelevant. Caroline Eves, who has directed extensively in repertory and in alternative theatre, commented on her experience:

I think now that sometimes where I used to put problems

down just to difference of opinion, it was often also to do
with me being a woman. I think women directors have to
prove themselves far more than men. I was refused a job
once when I was pregnant – they got a lady member of the
board to ring me up and ask me if I could cope.

She carried her perceptions about sexism back into her repertory
work, using available resources to subvert the usual assumptions
behind local pantomime:

I've just done one play in which the women's parts were just
cyphers and it was very hard. But I gave some of the men's
parts to women, which is often an easy thing to do – like
doctors, lawyers. And I did a pantomime, *Sinbad the Sailor*.
I worked quite closely with the writer (a man) and we did it
so that it was Sinbad's wife who was good at sailing, and
every time there was a home scene she'd be charting a course
on the map and he'd be sweeping the floor or something.
We didn't make any comment about it, we just did it.

Women directors who are sensitive to feminism can thus have an
important freelance role in showing theatre companies positive
alternatives:

I went to work in a theatre company and I said that the
company must be half men and half women. There's a
generation of men in their mid-forties who've done some
very good work, but who cannot believe a theatre can work
with a company that's fifty-fifty. One director said: 'If I take
on more women there would be even less work for them
to do because of the plays I have to put on.' I said, 'Well,
why don't you put on a show next that has an all-female
cast?' and he simply hadn't thought of it. It's not that he's
particularly hostile, he just didn't understand how it could
work.

(Caroline Eves)

In the day-to-day rehearsal a woman director needs to confront
the assumption that authority can only be male, and that the way
women are expected to behave in society must be reflected in a
woman director's behaviour:

It's very annoying because you hear actors talking about
'difficult' male directors with a tone of admiration. 'Oh,
he's a difficult man, but he's a good director.' I get so sick
of them wanting women to be nice and understanding and
make you feel it's wrong to lose your temper.

(Sue Dunderdale)

Women directors are also in a position to alter assumptions that
affect the artistic process of rehearsal:

I was devising a show with a company and the women got
very upset with the male actors because they thought the
men were being too creative and overshadowing them. And
I kept saying, 'You're got to be more outgoing and fight
them, you can't play the victim onstage.'

(Sue Dunderdale)

The trouble is you're fighting the fact that the women are
brought up to service and cherish. In improvisations I
always have to check that the girls don't always get up and
make the coffee.

(Caroline Eves)

And this conditioning is something which can also be present
for the woman director:

many of the roles that a female director plays are described
as mothering ones. Joan Littlewood is well known for
having called and treated her company as children, and
descriptions of her by her company abound in images of
an all-powerful, extraordinary, loving, terrifying mother-
figure. Many directors compare their nurturing role in
rehearsal with that of a mother, or see themselves as a kind
of nanny in relation to the actors – and this image of the
female role in rehearsal is one shared by mothers and non-
mothers alike.

The image is a limiting one in that it confines artistic
relationships inside the stereotypes of what is 'known' about
women. Men are strong leaders, women aren't strong leaders,
but – ah! mothers are leaders to their children, ergo it's
okay to be mother-leaders. To use the 'mother' image makes

leadership respectable for women perhaps, but it also encourages a queasy archetype which maintains women as proponents of the 'gentle' arts, defines them again only in relation to others, and so contains their rebellion.

(Clare Venables, *op. cit.*)

Designers

In an exhibition of Contemporary Theatre Design held at Riverside Studios, London, in 1979, twenty-seven of the sixty-four designers were women. Theatre design has, in the twentieth century, attracted women, in part because of the links between interior decor and the elaborate naturalistic indoor sets of nineteenth-century proscenium drama. Designer Di Seymour commented: 'For a long time design was a pretty effect at the back of the stage. In old programmes it was "set decorator".'

Today's alternative theatre with its limited resources has made theatre design cover the whole process – from the drawing board to the actual construction of the set. In larger theatres the process is broken down much further, till in very big theatres the top designer can cling entirely to the 'artistic' side of the work, drawing and making a model of the design, but not necessarily seeing it through the workshops. In the production process as a whole, the designer often takes on a kind of chameleon role: sometimes interpretative artist, sometimes technical chargehand. Through alternative theatre women designers have inevitably entered the 'male' world of manual work, and this has rebounded on their perceptions of the more traditional functions of theatre designer:

> In the big theatres you have more overall artistic authority because there are more resources to back up your decisions, but you have less practical control; with the smaller companies you have the satisfaction of working creatively with other people, but you're always limited by the budget.
>
> (Di Seymour)

The designer on the one hand services the director and the production, and on the other supervises the technical side of construction. Although women are far more accepted as designers than in any of the other 'creative' skills, there is still prejudice which stems from the sexual as well as the social division of labour:

> I think that people sometimes feel that there is a conflict between the practical person and the thinker; I mean, the director is the thinker, the one with the vision, and he forgets that the designer has to think as well. It is interesting that it does still seem to divide up along male/female lines; like the female is the practical one and the male is the thinker.
>
> (Di Seymour)

> I wanted a set done with metal, and there was this carpenter and he was thinking, 'I've never worked with metal before', so I put the helmet and goggles on and started showing him how to do it. He didn't like that at first but he got over it. The thing is, you're forced into doing things like that and making them into a strong statement as a woman, not because you want to but because the situation makes you aware that welding is not considered typically women's work.
>
> (Mary Moore)

Although working as a theatre designer involves a range of craft skills – from the 'soft' skills of dressmaking to the 'hard' skills of welding – the gender of a designer can at times make a difference:

> I think women have a different attitude to being confided in. But then I don't know how a male director might moan to a male designer. There is one very well-known director who has a tradition of always employing women designers, and he respects you very much as a designer. But step outside that and the discrimination starts. He was doing a documentary show, and I said I didn't think there were enough women's parts and the ones there were were being portrayed rather stupidly. And he said, 'Don't give me all this Women's Lib stuff, you're here to design, not to make comments like that.' It got to the stage where if I was in a room with another woman he would accuse us of gossiping. But that's not him as a theatre director, that's him as a particular person who finds it hard to cope with women putting their point of view.
>
> (Mary Moore)

And, like women directors, women designers might have an ambivalent attitude towards ambition, which may go some way towards explaining why so few women designers become 'top' names:

> My agent tells me I'm not pushy enough to be a great designer. I do mind distress in people, and if someone is worried or has just had a baby, and that is affecting their work, then I do get involved. I feel sometimes that if I was a 'real man' I would just get in there . . . you know. With the real jet-setting designers, they can do a design which will create total havoc in the design department and it just slides through the system without their having to handle any of the problems. I couldn't do that.

> (Di Seymour)

Administration and technical production

In larger companies women are rarely found in top management; they remain at middle-management level, associated with casting, personnel and their traditional servicing, clerical and publicity roles. Again, in alternative theatre the administrator has to do the whole lot, dealing both with internal administration and liaising between the company and the world. Women administrators have found that their role is largely accepted, except when they are dealing with money. Banks and Regional Arts Associations appear to be more suspicious of women who come to talk to them about a company's financial needs – a demonstration of the double standard which assumes a woman can manage her household purse but loses all sense of proportion when she deals with money in public.

On the production and technical sides of theatre work things are perhaps most backward of all. Behind-the-scenes work, operating the lights, any job which demands skilled or semi-skilled manual effort, or technological or electrical expertise, is still very much the province of men. In larger theatres there is a strong distinction backstage between the 'creative' and 'non-creative' skills; lighting design is considered 'creative', whereas the more practical work, such as working the lighting board is not. Technicians in alternative theatre have blurred those distinctions to some extent.

Rony Wood trained as a technician in repertory theatres where often she was the only woman in an all-male crew. The process of proving herself involved having to work out an attitude to the basic assumption that women (unlike men) cannot lift heavy weights:

> There is this assumption that you should be able to lift something heavy because men can. With most things there's a knack of moving them anyway, which you can learn. But the men sort of expected you to be able to lift things – and the double bind was that you felt you had to, even though it was silly, even though you knew that if a man was dealing with a very big rostrum he would yell for someone to come and help.

Meri Jenkins, who had a wide range of production and stage management experience, amplified the contradictory position in which a woman doing a 'man's' job find herself:

> I found there were two extremes. You would either get someone saying, 'If you say you can do it, go on, do it. But you've got to do it better than me.' Or you would get, 'No, don't touch that, I'll do it.' That's the most enormous strain because it means you're fighting a running battle with yourself trying to work out a balance between the two extremes and trying to know where to draw the line between what you can do on your own and where you need help.

In certain circumstances men identify with the challenge of showing a woman can do a man's job: 'I think he actually took more care than he would if I'd been a bloke, because it became a matter of his pride that I should be very good.' (Rony Wood.)

Where the boundaries of the male stronghold are identifiable, women are accepted once they have proved themselves. However, there are problems, because acceptance can often be predicated on the women herself fitting into the male cultural association – being 'one of the lads'. This may be fine up to a point, but not all women want to take over male norms of behaviour, and some will actually want to challenge them. The token woman accepted by men is in a precarious position, both for herself and for what she may represent for all women – that is, she may be the exception who for men proves the rule. Women appear to meet with strongest prejudices at the top end of the authority/artistic scale, and at the base line of practical, production work. Where roles combine different qualities in the middle of the spectrum, resistance to the presence of women has points of weakness, and in those areas women can more easily find work.

Criticism

In simple, statistical terms theatre is a 'minority' art. Only about 2 per cent of the population go to the theatre. But in the longer term, the minority art can become available to mass audiences, through being transmitted on television, made into film, or published and being put on school or college reading lists. In the short term there is also a fair amount of cross-fertilisation within the profession itself. Performers, writers and directors move between 'alternative' and 'established' theatre, between theatre and television or radio work, and this process filters some of the grassroots radical work up to a wider audience. This filtering process can be aided or hindered by the national press critics; the majority of these (who are men) are in general hostile to the whole notion of political theatre, and particularly aggressive and presumptuous about feminist and gay work:

> Feminist theatre is apt to be self-conscious and didactic, eager to use the stage as a pulpit.
>
> (*The Stage*, 20 September 1979)

> This is feminist theatre without butch aggro and with a lot of style.
>
> (Michael Billington on *The Club*, *Guardian*, 16 May 1978)

These are random examples of men writing on feminism and theatre, in the process implying that women are dull, unfeminine and humourless. It would be very easy indeed to quote page after page of misogynist, impatient, intellectually lazy extracts from theatre reviews, interviews with women theatre workers, and articles about feminists working in the theatre. One particularly common ploy is for the male critic to respond to feminist criticism of male dominance in the theatre by reeling off a list of female characters (the Antigone syndrome) and a list of famous writers or directors (the why aren't you Lillian Hellman/Joan Littlewood syndrome). Many critics find it genuinely difficult to respond to plays about women's experiences, because to do so would entail recognising that this is different from the run of what most plays are about. Critic John Barber, writing in the *Telegraph* in 1982, first of all adopted the above tactics in order to dismiss any cause for complaint from women, and then announced:

> The truth is, women are particularly well equipped for the theatre. For generations the physically weaker sex have had to develop their sense of observation and of character, as well as their instinct for penetrating motives and for understanding the human, as distinct from the material, elements in a problem.

Women writers whose work is taken seriously are often personally dealt with awkwardly, or accorded the dubious tribute of patronising sexual flattery. In his introduction to a review of *Action Replay*, Tony Palmer commented: 'Fay Weldon is a dishy lady who writes sympathetically about women.' (*Kaleidoscope*, BBC Radio 4, 3 March 1979.) In the same programme Michael Billington, *Guardian* theatre critic, spoke regretfully of the danger of 'a gender ghetto where men write about men successfully and women write about women successfully'.

The irony is that these 'ghettos' already exist; one of the important functions of feminist and gay theatre work has been to reveal an already discriminatory situation, to create positive spaces where they can redress the balance and create new work which not only challenges but contributes a vital new element to existing theatre. Such a space has also built up new audiences, supported by criticism from sympathetic areas of the press: the daily *Morning Star*, the weekly *Time Out*, the fortnightly *Gay News* and *Tribune*, and the monthly *The Leveller* and *Spare Rib*. The main function of criticism in these publications has been informative and supportive, and although this sometimes can lead to too much uncritical support, it is still preferable to the ignorance or prejudice which is still, with few exceptions, the dominant tone of the national press.

It is certainly true that the gay press and the cultural magazines which take particular account of fringe theatre (*Time Out* and *City Limits* in London) have provided the greatest service in disseminating information and in providing sympathetic coverage of gay and women's work. There is of course a problem here in that sometimes, in the interests of promoting the new, some critical judgement is suspended. This is an accusation often thrown at 'alternative' criticism. But it needs to be seen in context, and perhaps something of my own experience is relevant here. I wrote theatre reviews, articles, etc. for *Time Out* for eleven years, 1971–82, and looking back through my cuttings, I notice an interesting pattern. In the early years the novelty of anything by or about women seized me with great enthusiasm. It was very energetic work, and any aesthetic roughness round the edge was more than compensated for by the electricity of the company's energy; audiences were avid for work which presented women's and/or gay experience. Those of us who reviewed this work shared in the excitement, and it was quite the opposite of a 'ghetto' sensation. It was as if the world of theatre was opening up, just as it had in the late 1960s with visits over here of the American Living Theatre and many other groups.

As my reviewing progressed through the 1970s, I sensed a growing dilemma: while I was still absolutely supportive of anything which placed women's or gay experience centre stage, I began to feel that the history we were making demanded a more stringent critical response. And yet these shows all depended on 'good' reviews, especially from the 'alternative' press, in order to get their audiences. The theatre critic is not just an analyst or an arbiter of taste, but has an important function in the cycle of production-distribution-consumption of theatre. A critical review may be accurate, spot-on, but if it puts audiences off seeing the play, the company's livelihood is put in jeopardy. I developed two kinds of tactic for this: I found ways of suggesting critical comments in the context of a largely supportive review, and I became more cautious about what I reviewed. In a number of cases I declined to review a play, leaving it to someone whose palate was perhaps a little less jaded, and whose enthusiasm could come to the fore.

The revised edition of this book, which you are now reading, is also part of that historical process. When I was writing the first version, in 1978–80, the volume of work was such that I felt the most important thing was to document as factually as possible, raising occasional questions, and being sparing on the critical analysis. This time it has seemed to me that the history has something of a firm foothold, and that since so many vague clichés abound about the nature of feminist/gay theatre, a mixture of documentation and commentary can be more evenly balanced, since the future of healthy criticism must be based on a thoroughly understood and debated history.

The rest of this book is about playwrights, and it has a number of aims: first of all, to present an informative, critical evaluation of the work of some of the women playwrights whose plays have appeared in the past fifteen years. Secondly, to do the same for the (mainly male) gay playwrights. Thirdly, to look briefly at the way in which male playwrights through the 1970s tried to respond to the critiques feminists were making of male dominance in the content of theatre. Fourthly, to suggest some of the important ways in which the 'radical' drama of the 1970s and 1980s differs from its precursors in the 1950s and 1960s, and fifthly, to suggest a critical framework which will encourage discussion and greater understanding about the ways in which feminism has influenced contemporary writing – in other words, to demonstrate the way politics and art engage in a dialogue through the relationship between feminism and theatre. In order to set up the terms of the discussion, two things are necessary: an understanding of the way in which women writers fit into the context of play-writing, and a proper understanding of the nature of the new feminism of the 1970s.

7

Finding a voice: women playwrights and theatre

Women writers have been formative in the development of the novel as a literary genre. With the rise of a leisured class in the eighteenth century, the occupation of novel-writing (and the more 'private' forms of diary- and letter-writing) was taken up by these new ladies of leisure. Their contemporary reading public also consisted largely of such women, writing and reading in private, leaving the public world of book publishing and distribution to men. As Victorian attitudes to women hardened in the nineteenth century, women novelists, whose work had become more important, had a contradictory situation to deal with. Their work was being published and widely read and acclaimed, but the very fact that they were women called for censure – the use of the male pseudonym was a response to a double standard: the work was in demand but there was misogynistic resentment at the women writing it. Such women were transgressing the Victorian belief that womanhood should be a passive vocation in itself.

Since the end of the nineteenth century, as all the professions extended opportunities to women, the woman novelist and poet has been less of an anomaly. In this century women novelists have a relatively secure place as producers of fiction, although if they speak up outside the confines of their fiction as feminists they are likely to meet with hostility from the media.

As playwrights, however, women scarcely figure on the literary map. American feminist Eleanor Batchelor, in her introduction to a bibliography of plays by women commented: 'We have had relatively few women who were first and foremost playwrights . . .' (*Plays By Women*, Womanbooks, 1977, p. 1) Feminist research is revealing far more submerged work by women playwrights, some of which was acclaimed in its own time, but has since been forgotten. Aristocratic women had written plays for courtly masques, but it was not until actresses appeared on the Restoration stage in the late seventeenth century that women began writing for the stage professionally – the best known of these being Aphra Behn, who is popularly known as Britain's first professional woman playwright. The ambiguous position which women held in the theatre in those early days also extended to her; she was respected for her art and her politics, but she also represented a threat, as a woman who was economically and sexually independent – that is, more like a 'man' than a 'woman' and gossip reviled her for her supposed immorality, where it ignored the same behaviour in men.

But it is hard to think offhand of a really well-known woman playwright in the twentieth century. Writers such as Lilian Hellman and Doris Lessing have written plays, but they are as well, if not better, known by their work as novelists. Historically, women have been more in evidence as playwrights at moments of social and cultural change (for example, during the Restoration, in the early part of the twentieth century, and the 1970s), as a small minority, disappearing when the social crisis is over. Women have often written plays alongside another theatrical career, for instance, as actress or director. Many of the plays written for the Actresses' Franchise League (founded in 1908) were written by the actresses themselves because there was no other material. Later, in the 1930s sisters Angela and Joan Tuckett wrote and produced plays on women's rights as part of Unity Theatre's socialist theatre programme.

Although women have written for the theatre more in the last fifteen years, we are still in a minority. *Contemporary Dramatists* (St James' Press, 1977) selected by an advisory board of thirty-two men and one woman, is a compendious volume listing 321 playwrights working in English throughout the world. Of these thirty-four are women (under 10 per cent of the total) of whom fourteen work in England. The *British Alternative Theatre Directory*[1] will include any playwright who wants to be listed; out of 327 playwrights in 1980 only thirty-eight were women. The 1983 edition reveals a slight change – out of 547 playwrights listed, 103 are women. Many of these playwrights also write for other media

– radio, television – but the book is a good indicator of those playwrights who consider themselves working professionals who want to put (or keep) themselves on the theatrical map. The fact that the figure has risen from just over 10 per cent to just under 20 per cent represents a number of things – that more people are aware that the directory exists and have therefore sent in information about themselves, and that women playwrights take themselves more seriously and have hopes that the theatre world will too.

Whereas the above book is self-selecting, a different pattern emerges when one looks at the ratio of women writers to men represented in the catalogues of the major drama publishers, for both the professional and the amateur market. Methuen's list of plays in print in 1980 had one woman (plus one as a co-writer) out of forty modern British stage playwrights published. In their 1985 catalogue, Methuen's list of twentieth-century playwrights, who are accorded the privilege of having their plays published in single volumes (the 'prestige' end of commercial play publishing), consists of eighty writers, of whom seven are women, plus one woman as co-writer. Eleven more women writers are published in the anthologies which I have edited[2] and a further three in other anthologies. In 1980, out of thirty-five playwrights published, Faber could only include one woman.

Samuel French's 1979 'Plays for Performance' are listed in two catalogues: their 'Plays for Women' runs to thirty-two pages; their 'Plays for Men' to a mere nine. In the former booklet eighty-two writers are listed, of whom twenty-eight are women, and in the latter forty-two writers, of whom only four are women.

Samuel French's 1984 catalogue reveals that in their section of full-length plays for mixed casts, there are a total of 418 writers, of whom thirty-four are women; a further nine women are co-writers. One-act plays, also for mixed casts, show a total of 152 writers, of whom thirty-one are women, with one woman as co-writer. Of the nineteen full-length plays with all-women casts, six are by women writers. One-act plays for all-female casts boast a total of 138 plays, of which sixty are by women, with one woman as a co-writer. There are nineteen full-length plays for all-male casts, all written by men; and twenty-nine one-act plays for all-male casts, of which three are by women. The section covering plays, monologues and sketches for women performers only runs to forty-six pages, and the equivalent for men performers only to twenty pages. One more statistic: in Methuen's 1985 catalogue, information is given for the majority of plays as to the male-female ratio of the characters. Without allowing for the doubling that is possible in some plays, the plays contain parts for 2,212 male characters and for 908 female characters, which means there are roughly two-and-a-half male characters to each female character.

Making sense of these statistics produces some very interesting conclusions about the ways in which women playwrights are distributed, in respect of the different theatrical markets: first of all, where simple, professional self-selection is involved, nearly 20 per cent of the listed playwrights are women. However, when it comes to the top 'professional' selection by the country's leading publisher for the general market, the number drops to below 10 per cent, and although that figure is up on the 1980 catalogue, it is still scandalously low. (The playwrights who appear in anthologies are usually there because they fit into the themes of the anthologies; the real publishing accolade is to be given an individual volume; I can't resist adding here that I consider a number of the plays I have included in my *Plays by Women* anthologies as far superior to many of the other plays accorded this accolade by the publisher.) In the survey referred to in Chapter 6 it was found that only about 7 per cent of all produced plays in the theatres covered were by women, and of these, productions of Agatha Christie plays accounted for half. While things have clearly improved a little in the five years between 1980 and 1985, there is still a long way to go before the number of available women playwrights is accurately reflected in the percentage of plays produced and published – and still further to go before plays by contemporary women represent 50 per cent of theatrical output.

Turning to the plays aimed largely at the amateur market, the picture is different: first of all, the number of plays for all-female casts is nearly two-and-a-half times that for all-male casts. The amateur theatre world is clearly dominated by women simply in numbers, if this figure is anything to go by – a most interesting counterpoint to the professional theatre. The amateur market is still dominated by male playwrights, but it is interesting that women have almost reached 50 per cent where they write one-act plays for all-female casts. At the other end of this particular scale, they have written none of the full-length plays for all-male casts, and well under 10 per cent of full-length plays for mixed casts – the largest category in the catalogue. We can conclude from this that women playwrights find the greatest outlet for their work (a) in the amateur market; (b) in writing one-act plays for all-female casts, and are least likely to have plays on the market (a) for full-length, mixed casts and; (b) for all-male casts.

Male dominance is common in both the professional and amateur markets, and it seems clear that women seem to be more inclined to write about their own sex (and for their own sex to perform) rather than to write about men; male playwrights clearly do not feel themselves limited, but do (if we are to judge from the Methuen cast-list breakdown) tend to produce plays heavily biased towards their own sex in terms of the number of male characters. Men are just as biased towards writing about their own sex as women are, but show this in a slightly different way. Women also seem to have chosen the shorter form – the one-act play, in preference to the larger canvas of the full-length play. However, this could be one of those chicken-and-egg situations, where the full-length plays which are then channelled towards the amateur market are already more likely to be by men (men being more successfully performed in the professional theatre), and many women may content themselves with writing one-act plays precisely because the amateur market has a great hunger for them (as well as through the influence of television and the fact that fringe theatre has encouraged shorter plays). These figures show where and how women are distributed in the play-writing sphere, but one should be cautious before drawing crude conclusions; what is clear is that there is a process of dilution going on, and that women are clustered in the least prestigious and least remunerative areas of play-writing, and this disadvantages them professionally.

Theatre is plainly a difficult field for women to write in; there are a number of reasons for this. Firstly, there is a clear link between the fact that men dominate the economic and artistic decisions in theatre and the way that women are represented as characters in plays. The content of plays is ideologically 'policed' far more explicitly than the content of novels, because of the difference in the way the genres are produced and distributed. The novel, for example, remains intact as an artefact once it is published. By contrast the play as a 'text' takes two forms: as a 'text-in-performance' – the live theatrical event, the success of which will determine whether or not a play reaches publication. If it does then become a 'published text', it does so having already been sanctioned by decisions made by the live theatre. A playwright could, of course, write a play in the proverbial garret and then take no interest in how it is produced onstage. But in general people choose to write plays because they are interested in seeing them staged, and in experiencing the satisfaction of seeing their words brought alive in performance.

Writing for the theatre offers the combination of the individual creative process with the benefits of collaborative work, even if the writer is not always present in rehearsal. But on the whole the playwright must in a sense 'come out' more publicly than the novelist: s/he cannot hide behind a safely published text, and (particularly in rehearsal) s/he is vulnerable to the scrutiny and demands of co-workers – director, performer, etc. Play-writing is so much more public an art than novel- or poetry-writing that it demands more from all writers; for women the demands are doubled, since they also have to deal with the (not always conscious) assumptions that women are not capable of public, artistic responsibility. The playwright is public in two important senses: her/his name is likely to be visible in large letters outside a theatre, to be prominent in advertisements. And with the tradition (ironically enhanced in the days of censorship) that the theatre is in some way a subversive, potentially inciteful medium, the critical establishment is always looking to its theatre writers to produce the public, radical voice of dissent, in some way to give public voice to social comment, satire, criticism. One only has to follow the way in which the press sees new plays by the current generation of 'angry young men' as a comment on our times, to see how authoritative the voice of the playwright is often expected to be.

For a woman writer to take on this role of authoritative voice means that in some implicit way she is combating the dominant image of women in the theatre – and, as outlined in Chapter 2, this image is hedged in by the invisible, servicing female on the one hand, and by the visible, glamorous, or sexually desirable female on the other. Of course, there is always the exception – the 'serious' actress, or the occasional important woman playwright, but these exceptions also serve to reinforce the rule. In theory, of course, the time is long past when women were denied credit as writers, but I believe that because the theatre has lagged so far behind the novel and poetry in its acceptance of women as writers, attitudes, which critic Cora Kaplan has placed in the nineteenth century, are still present in the consciousness of the theatre:

> The taboo, it is stronger than prejudice, against women's entry into public discourse as speakers or writers, was in grave danger of being definitively broken in the mid-nineteenth century as more and more educated, literate women entered the arena as imaginative writers, social critics and reformers. . . . Public writing and public speech, closely allied, were both real and symbolic acts of self-determination for women.
>
> (Introduction to reprint of *Aurora Leigh*, by Elizabeth Barret Browning, The Women's Press, 1978, p. 9)

A woman writer is reacted to as a *woman* as much or sometimes more than she is as a *writer*; in a culture which values the received traditions of 'great' literature as much as ours does, a woman writer who has greatness thrust on her also has to pass in some way as a woman, in terms of her social/sexual behaviour. A woman writer has more than a man to overcome before she can be accepted as an artistic 'equal' in the theatre.

The other reason that women have not chosen to write so readily for the theatre relates to play-writing as a form. Writing plays involves finding a voice: not only in developing a distinct and individual literary style and 'voice', but also because it entails writing in dialogue, which even in its most contemplative moments is an active social art. After all, even a soliloquy consists of an individual talking ostensibly to her/himself but in fact doing so in public, communicating to an audience. Also, even the most static play involves conflict or dilemma and its resolution in some form, and women are much less accustomed than men to acknowledging and dealing with conflict in public. It is not that women are strangers to conflict, but that women are accustomed to dealing with conflict in the privacy of the home – behind closed doors – and within relationships between individuals, rather than in larger groups. The cultural roots of women's experiences are not those of public social struggle or political power – and it is thus not surprising that women have rarely contributed to the development of epic drama, particularly when such drama deals with the realities of politics in which government by and conflict between men is the norm. It is also not surprising that the naturalist/realist theatre which developed from the end of the nineteenth century coincided with the changes in the situation of women, in which the site of the action is shifted to the home, although still largely in terms of the dilemmas which concern men. The domestic and interpersonal conflicts with which women are familiar are simply not seen as important, compared with the concerns of men.

The language of a play, then, consists of dialogue (or monologue, but in any case speech) and action (stage directions or implied action) in which the playwright is controlling (quite literally) the voices of others. She is providing words, emotions, and an imaginative structure for others to inhabit and create anew onstage. A playwright – in this theoretical sense – thus makes other people speak and act – an act of public responsibility and control which is very rare indeed for women in other parts of society. No wonder, then, that even the women playwright with the mildest of messages is bound to be seen as an anomaly, if not an actual threat. Who knows what she will say once she gives voice? Who knows what she will tell other people to say and do? And it is precisely this extraordinary range of potential voice and subject matter which makes the advent of women writers into theatre both so necessary and so exciting.

In keeping with the presence of women playwrights in the less visible areas of drama, women have contributed significantly to radio drama. The British Broadcasting Corporation is the largest single commissioner of plays in the world, and radio drama has developed its own intimate forms, in keeping with the fact that it is listened to at home, alone. For obvious reasons radio has a high proportion of women listeners (the Afternoon Theatre slot has over twice as many female as male listeners), and the relatively large number of women writing for radio has parallels with the women writer-reader relationship in the eighteenth century, and with the amateur theatre movement today. Radio is also far less in the public eye, and radio drama has an established tradition of working

closely with writers in a context where the writer can watch
production but is far less exposed than in the longer and more
open rehearsal periods in theatre. Playwright Gilly Fraser who
began by writing for radio comments on the link between woman
as writer and woman as listener:

> I remember before I started writing when I was housebound
> with four kids and very frustrated, radio in the afternoon
> saved my life. So what comes out when I write is what it's
> like to be female – and that's being conveyed to women in
> the same state as I was, who'd never go to the theatre.
>
> (Interview with Anne Karpf, *Time Out*, 12–18 October
> 1979)

8

Political dynamics: the feminisms

Because of the scarcity value of women playwrights, and of plays which take either a female-gendered perspective, or which are largely or entirely about women, it is all too easy sometimes for them to be casually labelled with one of the many new clichés which have sprung up during the 1970s: 'feminist theatre', 'women's theatre', 'plays for women' – all these convey some important clue as to the bias or content of a play, but they are not analytical. They are useful signposts; but they can be used by misogynists in order to sneer at and ghettoise new work by and about women. Or they can be used in a blanket sort of way to imply support and approval (nothing wrong with that) and to forestall any criticism or comment. It seems to me both exciting and important to try to understand precisely the way in which the ideas generated through political feminism have affected (or not) the work of women and men playwrights. We are, after all, talking about the complex ways in which imaginative work is both a product of its own time, and a response to it, and writing a work of fiction (in this case, a play), even if it has documentary sources, is an engagement with the relationship between the conscious knowledge and ideas of the writer, and the way s/he then digests that knowledge and creates a fictional, imaginative world. This imaginative world cannot simply be 'checked off' against 'reality'. It is an act of illusion, since it creates its own internal rules, it is part of a tradition – or traditions – whether the writer is aware or not, and it constantly alludes to empirically verifiable bits of the real world, and to the imaginations and emotions of its audiences. There is no simple way in which neat correlations between politics and art (feminism and theatre) can be made; but it is essential that some attempt is made, in order to understand the plays better. It is not a game to pass abstract value judgements; after all, we all tend to like what we agree with, and we will all continue to be inspired and moved by different things. We are all familiar with the experience of going to the theatre with someone and then finding that we have diametrically different views about what was good, what was moving, or even, sometimes, what the play was about.

First of all, some clarification on the nature of feminism. Or rather, of the feminisms. Feminism is not a crude or a homogeneous thing. It has a history (a number of histories, indeed) and has taken different forms at different times. Having said that, it is important to stress that just because a play is by a woman, or includes women characters, or has an all-female cast, it does not necessarily mean that the play will be sympathetic to feminism, even though it may be about emotions and actions which are not commonly seen on the stage. Because a play is about women does not necessarily mean that it is about feminism; and if it is, it is important to try to understand how it refracts its feminist influences. For the purposes of this discussion, I have limited the description of feminism to its three major tendencies – as they have emerged during the 1970s. There are of course other gradations, and there are overlaps between the three tendencies, but they each stem from a different theoretical explanation of why women are where they are in society, and they each have a different set of political and tactical priorities for responding to the analysis, and bringing about social change. The three tendencies share three important features: (1) All three tendencies seek to bring about some sort of change in the position of women. (2) All three tendencies challenge both the idea and the fact of male dominance. (3) All three tendencies assert the importance of self-determination for women. However, each tendency interprets this principle, at both the personal/individual and the social/collective levels, in different ways. But they do all challenge the crudeness of a biological determinism that says that women are biologically weaker than, and inferior to, men, and that women's social and cultural inferiority therefore follows on. All three feminisms, then, challenge the oppressiveness of different aspects of the social/sexual division of labour. It should be clear from this that not all women are necessarily feminists (women who do not want to change anything, for example), though all feminists must necessarily be women. Men cannot be feminists, although they can, and importantly should be encouraged (challenged?), to support feminism, participate in the struggle against sexism in a variety of ways, and change themselves in the process. The chief reason why it is wrong to define anti-sexist men as feminists is because of the self-determination component in the consciousness and practice of women; to become self-determining for a woman means taking some kind of action against an identity which she has received from her social conditioning – i.e., the identity of the so-called inferior sex. Men do not receive such conditioning – the reverse; they may, of course, be dissatisfied with their own 'conditioned', 'masculine' identity, but their response to that will be on the basis of their gendered experience as men who refuse an image of macho superiority, not of the gendered experience of women who refuse an identity of inferiority. Men are already encouraged to be far more self-determining than women – and the subject matter of this book is living proof of how that works in the theatre.

The three kinds of feminism, then:

1 Radical feminism

Radical feminism springs from the direct, gut response of all women to the day-to-day irritations and resentments which women feel and experience. Radical feminism articulates these responses, analyses and politicises the details of oppression. It challenges very directly the notion that men are biologically superior to women, and it does so by claiming that what women do and think and feel is socially valuable and important. Radical feminist theory argues that the oppression of women predates capitalism, and that therefore all subsequent forms of social injustice stem from the basic sexual antagonism between men and women. Thus for radical feminism 'men' (i.e. biological and social maleness) are seen as the primary enemy, and everything that is 'bad' in the world (i.e. war, aggression) is seen as 'male', and everything 'good', (caring, nurturing) is seen as 'female'. It will be seen that radical feminism simply inverts the model of sexist values, and produces a reverse moral system, in which – instead of men on top and women below – women are on top and men are below.

Radical feminism is thus a crucially significant thing, but also very contradictory. It has important active aspects, and dangerous passive aspects. Active radical feminism encourages women to unite, to develop solidarity on the basis of their gender; it asserts that women are strong and powerful, and not feminine and weak; it refuses sexual passivity and objectification and exploitation by men, and it encourages women to become sexually self-determining, whatever their sexual orientation.

[However, in its passive aspects it connotes women as simply passive victims of a monolithic patriarchal system, producing an uncritical view of all women as good and pure (the alternative 'morality' as described above); and this, ironically, begins to sound and feel very like one of the very feminine stereotypes which radical feminism has sought to overthrow – the pure and blameless ideal which is enshrined in the feminine image of the good madonna. Radical feminism offers a dualist analysis of social structure divided simply along gender lines, and this position leads to the very crude view that there is such a thing as a 'women's culture' and a 'women's language' which is entirely separate from that of men. The seductive but inaccurate notion that our language has been 'made' by men with no meanings for women, would, if taken to its logical conclusion, mean that men and women would never understand one another. It is more accurate to say that men have more power over some aspects of the language, and it is that power which women challenge.]

It is of course true that in a common-sense, everyday way, one often feels that men and women talk a different 'language'; but when such idiomatic expression is used instead of real cultural analysis, a very dangerous thing happens. In theatre, for example, such a view can be used to justify the idea that plays about women have no interest or relevance for men; that they are, in fact, 'for' women alone. In effect, this means that men are let off the hook, both as theatre workers and as members of the audience. They can shrug off what women are saying, and the forms their imaginations take, instead of being challenged on the grounds of their own ignorance and prejudice. It may be true (it often is) that women in the audience of a play about women are more likely to understand or respond to what they are seeing, but that does not mean that men can't. It means quite simply that men are being asked to recognise that they cannot assume that their imaginations can speak for women; and that women are challenging them not just to think about women differently, but also to think about themselves differently as men.

Because of its dualist gender philosophy, and its hostility to anything that it defines as essentially 'male', radical feminism has little or no interest in any class analysis, and no desire or interest in any political relationship with socialism or the labour movement, or any of the left-wing groups and parties.

2 Bourgeois feminism or emancipationism

Bourgeois feminism is a curious phenomenon; in a sense it has only become widespread and visible in the past five years or so – in the 1980s, in fact, although there were little pockets of it around in the 1970s. But the 1980s have made bourgeois feminism visible and respectable. Basically bourgeois feminism simply seeks a larger share of social power for a small number of women – the 'women at the top' syndrome. It often takes the apparently liberal line of 'men and women are different, but can be equal', but in practice this usually means that the real basis of power relations between the sexes (personal and political) is concealed. Bourgeois feminism accepts the world as it is, and sees the main challenge for women as simply a matter of 'equalling up' with men; in other words, what men already do is seen as the norm. Bourgeois feminism also has a little touch of radical feminism in there with this approach: unlike radical feminism, it does not challenge many of the aspects of femininity with which women are lumbered. The reverse. It asserts that women, if they really want to, and try hard enough, can make it to the top, and they have added strength because they can use their feminine wiles to twist men round their little fingers on the way there; thus they reveal a curious combination of total acceptance of men as the norm, together with an element of contempt for the sexual weakness of men who can be subject to the lures and power of flirtation and women's sexual power. This produces an odd hybrid: bourgeois radical feminism, in which women simultaneously depend on men and despise them, something which is very rooted in everyday experience, but which the bourgeois feminist turns to her own particular power advantage.

In other respects, however, bourgeois feminism is very different indeed from radical feminism: it places total stress on individual effort, which produces the token woman surrounded by men, and served by other women; this means that bourgeois feminism has no interest in any idea of solidarity or sisterhood – the reverse, since such an idea is bound to conflict with the notion of individual self-advancement. And because bourgeois feminism accepts the status quo (with a bit more power for women) it also – like radical feminism – has no interest in a class analysis, and certainly no interest whatsoever in socialism or the labour movement.

However, like radical feminism it has important strengths: it is absolutely straightforward about the importance of women taking responsibility for power. It stresses the need for women to take charge of territories normally seen as the 'male' preserve, and in its emphasis on the individual, it provides a model (or an image) for woman as an existential being, and as a responsible agent determining her own life and development. The concept of self-determination is thus taken up by bourgeois feminism in a way that is indeed contradictory, but which does carry with it the notion that we have to function as responsible individuals, whatever our social context or our politics.

One recent development shows how bourgeois feminism is becoming more and more influential in theatre in the 1980s, and that is the way that many women use the term 'actor' as if it were the generic term which includes 'actress' as part of its meaning. This is actually a retrograde step, since there is a very real gender distinction necessary in describing male and female performers, and to allow the word 'actor' to be the 'norm' is to help perpetuate the unconscious assumption that the actress is some kind of secondary or divergent category. In fact there is a perfectly good generic term, which is the one I have used throughout this book where relevant, and that is 'performer', which after all is the best general description of the job. Within that there are various subcategories, of which 'actor' and 'actress' are two, where one is referring to a male or a female performer; there are also other kinds of theatrical function, such as dancer, acrobat, etc., which are perfectly well accepted in common use, and which do not have the fraught hierarchical implications of the generic and bourgeois feminist term 'actor'. It is significant that it is in the theatre, in the performance of plays with words, in the use of language which controls explicit meaning, that the gender hierarchy of performers has been retained. Not to be recommended.

3 Socialist feminism

Socialist feminism draws together elements from the kind of class analysis developed by Karl Marx and others since, and the radical feminism which developed in the early 1970s. In terms of its theory, it aims to analyse and understand the way in which power relations based on class interact with power relations based on gender – again, at both the individual and the social level. Socialist feminism recognises that there are times and issues over which solidarity between women can cut across class or cultural barriers, but it also recognises the importance of struggles based on class, which necessarily involve men, and that women can have important differences among themselves, based on class difference.

Theoretically and strategically, socialist feminism is more far-reaching than either bourgeois or radical feminism; where radical feminism proposes a real surge of energy and solidarity between women, it does so by devaluing and ignoring men; bourgeois feminism values social power for women, but has no concern for class issues, and is still absolutely defined by men as the norm. Socialist feminism, on the other hand, proposes changes both in the position of women as women, and in the power relations of the very basis of society itself – its industrial production, and its political relations. Thus while radical and bourgeois feminism can account for certain kinds of reform change for women, only socialist feminism can offer an analysis which provides for genuine, revolutionary change.

Men can dismiss radical feminists as simply talking to themselves, and they can incorporate or co-opt the token bourgeois feminist into existing power structures; but only socialist feminism really challenges men both on their own territory and on territory they never knew existed. Men are challenged by socialist feminism on the basis of their class power, and their gender power – as male in a society which values the male higher than the female.

However, having said this, there are also contradictions within socialist feminism. For example, it is much harder to provide clear tactical steps; radical feminism can simply urge all women to ignore men and unite with other women, and can here find genuine, alternative ways of understanding the world and being. Bourgeois feminism can simply urge women to try harder as individuals. But socialist feminism has to ring the changes on the tactic of relative autonomy for women and the tactic of working together with men, and this is easier asserted in theory than outlined in practice. In a sense the socialist is always a kind of political cuckoo; among men her radical feminism is likely to assert itself when she challenges male dominance. Among women she is likely to plug the class analysis, to argue the case against simply blaming men for everything and assuming that there are no differences among women. There is also a strand of socialist feminism which comes from deep within the labour movement which has similarities to aspects of bourgeois feminism in its suspicion of radical feminist solidarity and women organising autonomously. But it is certainly true also that the traditional strengths of the socialist feminist position have been reinforced and given exciting new perspectives by the boldness and importance of radical feminism.

I would imagine that the reader will have gathered by the way I have approached these three feminist tendencies that my own political choice lies with the socialist-feminist. This does not mean that I am claiming that it is morally 'better' – indeed, as I have indicated, there are aspects of feminism which the other two tendencies are more able to confront clearly and head-on. The way I have approached this book has been on the basis of trying to develop a socialist-feminist analysis which can account for the place of women in theatre by referring both to the social and the sexual divisions of labour in theatre. It is also important to remember that the accounts of feminism which I have given are analytical, and do not correspond simply with the real life experience of every woman at every moment. In practice the political consciousness of any feminist is made up of all the various elements, with different aspects dominant in different women, and at different times. A feminist working in a very traditional theatre situation, where attitudes are very reactionary, is likely to find herself experiencing strong, gut, radical-feminist angers; a woman in a position of power in the theatre (as artistic director, say) has to face and deal with both her desires for power, and her actual objective power at work. And a feminist who is in a position to work democratically with others (say in a 'fringe' group) is more likely to be exploring ways of sharing power and control over work with others, with taking responsibility for herself and her work as a woman.

Since the feminist tendencies are complex, and since it is also impossible to make crude correlations between ideology, the individual and their objective situation, one must also approach the evaluation of plays from a political point of view with caution. In the analyses that follow I am not simply going to peel off labels with different tendencies on them and slap them on plays; there have been some attempts by women critics to define 'feminist theatre' or 'feminist plays', and in some cases this has ended up with a rather lame assertion that anything about women is necessarily feminist. As I shall show, this is not the case. I am interested in trying to evaluate the nature of the feminist dynamic – or in some cases the different feminist dynamics – operative in various plays. The feminist dynamics which I shall discern will be related to the tendencies I've discussed, but it will not result in a series of Good Housekeeping seals of approval or castigation. The relationship between the conscious idea in social circulation and what happens in the imagination of the writer is both too exciting and too important to be reduced to a political label. And yet the political analysis is absolutely essential, if we are to understand what it is that writers have been doing in the 1970s and 1980s. Where it is relevant, and has implications both for the actual production of plays discussed, and where it may be useful to raise it for future productions, I shall discuss context, performance, and the aesthetic implications of various styles of writing.

In order to place the work of the 1970s and 1980s in some kind of context, I have prefaced it with a brief look at some of the more important, radical plays of the 1950s and 1960s, with particular reference to the ways in which they imagined and placed women. Although the fact of feminism and the earlier feminist movement of the early part of the century were still very much in people's memories, and in the lives of many women who had lived through the suffragette movement, the 1950s and 1960s did not have a concerted, publicly visible, feminist movement. In relation to the feminism of the 1970s, these twenty years are 'pre-feminist', but what is interesting about the plays of these years is the way in which they prefigured so many concerns which 1970s feminism articulated and made explicit.

It is important to stress that the comments on individual plays are not intended as value judgements on the writers. One cannot assume that the views of a writer will be those of her/his main characters, or that every single play represents the whole of a writer's world view. Where it is relevant, I will make comments about a particular writer's preoccupations, insofar as they are evident from a group of plays by that writer.

As an introduction to a discussion of the plays of the 1970s, I shall briefly discuss the way in which sexual relations and the representation of women appeared in some of the radical plays of the 1950s. Bearing in mind the fact that political feminism was dormant during this period, these pre-feminist plays show how some of the more dissenting writers were grappling with women and the feminine, and with the 'female', as represented in relationships between women characters.

9

Radical plays before 1968: the crisis of virility, the 'feminine' and the 'female'

The 1950s

The new plays of the 1950s blew open the cosy assumptions of commercial drawing-room theatre. As has already been mentioned, it was very much a director-sponsored theatre; radical directors, exploring new methods, searched for new playwrights, as well as encouraging novelists or actors to write plays (both Arnold Wesker and John Osborne had been actors before becoming writers). Relatively radical though this new theatre was, it retained an unquestioned male bias. Even Joan Littlewood's energies at Stratford East went mainly into working with male writers, while in the twenty years from 1956–75 the Royal Court produced only seventeen plays (out of over 250) which were written and/or directed by women. Some of these 250 plays form the core of a canon of modern theatre classics, continually reprinted, on examination syllabuses, performed round the world. Some of them have been filmed and subsequently televised, so that what was once startlingly avant-garde, seen by a minority audience, is now accepted as a major contribution to twentieth-century drama, and has been seen by millions.

It is therefore worth re-examining some of the most successful of these plays, with the hindsight of a feminist perspective. The new class content of these plays was one of their most striking features, along with the development of a new social realism – the so-called 'kitchen-sink' school of theatre. This was actually a misnomer, with only a partial symbolic meaning; representing a move from the upper-middle-class drawing room to the working-

class settings of urban England, it very rarely turned its gaze on
the woman who might have been at the putative kitchen sink.
Instead the focus remained mainly on the men, but with a new
emphasis. Along with the changing class consciousness in these
plays went a sense of shift in gender and sexual roles. The way in
which men and manhood were represented began to change, and
with that came a contradictory but definitely new approach to the
representation of women.

Look Back in Anger: John Osborne

With this play in 1956 John Osborne created a new anti-hero,
whose barbed articulacy released a sense of bitter social criticism
with which many sympathised. The social and political climate of
the late 1950s was such that the complacencies of a new post-war
affluence were beginning to be challenged:

> It became impossible any longer just to dismiss politics as
> the uncouth squabbling over power from which a sensitive
> man would shrink. Politics hung over our lives in the
> threatening shape of a mushroom cloud. *Men* were either
> going to have to solve their problems or *cease to be men.*
> (my italics)
> (John Elsom, *Post-War British Theatre*, Routledge & Kegan
> Paul, 1979, p. 70)

Inadvertently, perhaps, John Elsom has hit on Jimmy's dilemma:
questions of manhood and virility are at stake for Jimmy as much,
if not more, than the state of the world. Jimmy laments that

> I suppose people of our generation aren't able to die for good
> causes any longer. We had all that done for us, in the
> thirties and the forties, when we were still kids.
> (*Look Back In Anger*, Faber, 1978, p. 84)

He is part of the new class-mobile generation of men who can still
identify the class enemy of dying imperialism, but have lost their
identification with their working-class roots, without finding (no
New Left yet) a new sense of collective identification. But his
political rage is displaced: firstly, his energies are expended totally

on his interpersonal relationships; and secondly, his sense of class hatred is sublimated into sexual hatred and venomous attacks on women in general and his wife Alison in particular. Suitably, Alison comes from the class he most despises, and his personal/political project in the play is to rediscover his own potency by destroying whatever vestiges of independence she has left. The destruction is intimate, sexual and verbally violent:

> do you know, I have never known the great pleasure of love-making when I didn't desire it myself. Oh, it's not that she hasn't her own kind of passion. She has the passion of a python. She just devours me whole every time as if I were some over-large rabbit. . . [That bulge around her navel – if you're wondering what it is – it's me. Me, buried alive down there and going mad.]

> (*Ibid.*, p. 37)

Quite early on in the play we learn that Alison is pregnant but scared to tell Jimmy; Alison is seen not only as sexually voracious, but as a vindictive mother who is preventing Jimmy from giving birth to himself, finding his meaningful identity as a man. Jimmy desires Alison's ultimate humiliation and wants her sexuality and capacity for motherhood simultaneously 'destroyed'. Consequently, when she returns to him at the end having lost the child she was carrying, he is quietly triumphant and hence able to be 'tender'.

Osborne's treatment of Alison is not entirely unsympathetic, but her structural function in the play is as a punchbag for Jimmy's discontent. When she leaves him we stay with Jimmy, rather than following her. She is thus not allowed space to develop as a character in her own right, and it is Jimmy's dilemma that is the central subject of the play, and Jimmy's sexuality that is under threat. Alison is humiliated by her author as well as by Jimmy; she is shown meekly doing housework, and her brief moment of rapport with Helena in Act Two is then undermined when Helena moves in with Jimmy in Act Three.

The 'sterility' of the Porters' marriage is highlighted by the function of Cliff, their friend and lodger. Cliff defends Alison and yet is totally trusted and loved by Jimmy. The significant physical contact actively enjoyed in the play is between Jimmy and Cliff –

two bouts of light-hearted wrestling. Although Cliff is statedly heterosexual, his stage presence is sexually neuter; he functions as a kind of 'child' in the distorted bedsitter family, and as an expression of a shadowy homo-erotic theme in the play. It is as though the play expresses some disturbance at the disintegration of the patriarchal family, but can only express this disturbance by offering a sublimated homosexual relationship between Jimmy and Cliff, or by displacing anger on to the woman/mother as the producer of man. If *Look Back in Anger* were simply a misogynist play it would not be worth much attention, but it is precisely because it is about the crisis of mid-twentieth-century virility that it is important.

A Taste of Honey: Shelagh Delaney

Shelagh Delaney's play was first produced by Joan Littlewood at the Theatre Royal, Stratford East, in 1958. Jo, a young working-class girl, is pregnant by her black boyfriend; she and her mother Helen row all the time, but understand each other extremely well; both are independent and resilient. When Helen leaves, Geoff, a homosexual art student, moves in with Jo. He looks after her, preparing for the baby in the face of her reluctance to accept potential motherhood, but when Helen has had enough of her sugar-daddy and returns, she throws Geoff out.

The play is rooted in domestic, female-centred experience: it opens with an abrasive exchange between Jo and Helen on arrangements in their new flat. At the centre of the play is Jo's attitude to womanhood; Geoff buys her a doll on which to practise, and she flings it from her, saying: 'I don't want to become a mother, I don't want to be a woman.' (*A Taste of Honey*, Eyre Methuen, 1975, p. 75.) Delaney's sense of the raw realities of working-class survival enables her to cut through all the conventional assumptions about sex and family life; she breaks racial taboos by showing an inter-racial sexual relationship, both Helen and Jo got pregnant by accident, and neither has any sentimentality about motherhood. Delaney, then, in this play, has no scruples in accepting a disintegrating family structure; she is pragmatic in showing alternative and non-moral ways in which women cope; when Helen returns and Geoff leaves, the two generations of women are together, living without men and not particularly bothered by that fact. Though heterosexual family life is problematic for them, they prefer to live without men rather than take their disillusion out on them.

At the same time the character of Geoff, like Cliff in *Look Back in Anger*, represents an area of sexual doubt which is left unexplored. Geoff is homosexual, more 'feminine' than Jo; but like Cliff, he has no sexual relationship within the play. Also like Cliff, he acts as a sexually neuter catalyst for the emotional dilemmas of the other characters, and when his services are no longer required, he exits. It is interesting that both Osborne and Delaney use a eunuch-like figure to act as an emotional catalyst for heterosexual dilemmas – and perhaps they were not fully conscious of what they were doing. The male 'eunuch' becomes a safe representation of maleness because he loses his sexuality in the process – another oblique symbol of the crisis of virility. However, the two plays treat pregnancy in different ways. For Delaney, writing as a woman, pregnancy is a real issue, and throws into question Jo's destiny and future life as a woman, whereas for Osborne pregnancy is symbolic, a threat to the man's potency in a woman's life.

Ann Jellicoe

The Sport of My Mad Mother (Royal Court, 1958) and *The Knack* (Royal Court, 1961) illustrate a difference between the male-female approaches in a theatrical form which is more abstract, surreal and verbally orchestrated. In Jellicoe's sophisticatedly schematic stage worlds, in which the concept of ritualised behaviour informs the minutiae of the action and dialogue, both Osborne's fearful look at threatened masculinity and the celebratory potential of motherhood reappear. *Sport* used the notion of myth as a point of departure; the play

> is concerned with fear and rage at being rejected from the womb or the tribe. It uses a very old myth in which a man, rejected by his mother, castrates himself with a stone knife.
> (Ann Jellicoe, *The Sport of My Mad Mother*, Faber, 1974, p. 5)

One of the characters, Greta, a pregnant girl, is beaten up, but at the end of the play she gives birth to a doll in a symbolic gesture of the continuation of life. *The Knack* also has a ritually stylised structure. The play is about Tolen, a young stud who lives out his belief that the world is divided into masters and servants:

> Very few men are real men, Colin, are real masters. Almost all women are servants. They don't want to think for themselves, they want to be dominated.
>
> (*The Knack*, Faber, 1979, p. 32)

The play is self-consciously about the mechanics of this male domination, exposing the macho games men play to vie with each other, revealing the intricacies of their domination through the nuances of everyday behaviour. Although Ann Jellicoe leaves her central woman character passive and largely inarticulate, she does so in order to demonstrate the nature of men's power-play in a way that focuses more explicitly on the qualities which define a man as 'a real man'.

Arnold Wesker

Chicken Soup with Barley (1958), *Roots* (1959) and *I'm Talking about Jerusalem* (1960) were first performed as a trilogy at the Royal Court in 1960. The action of the plays spans nearly thirty years – from the 1930s to 1959. They chart changes in socialist consciousness and activism mainly through the Kahns, a Jewish East End family with a tradition of trade union and Communist Party activism. Wesker retains the format of domestic realism, and despite the fact that we never see the demonstrations or political meetings which are so much a part of the family's history, everything that happens is redolent of a commitment to socialism as a way of life: 'Politics is living . . . I mean, everything that happens in the world has got to do with politics.' (Sarah Kahn, *The Wesker Trilogy*, Penguin, 1975, p. 61.)

Wesker's assertion of the positive and genuine values of socialism were in part a response to Communism's bad press in the 1950s – and he asserts these values even through the decline of Communist fervour in the 1950s. One figure carries the burden of proof of

these values through the trilogy – Sarah, the mother and pivot of
the family. Sarah is the most potent symbol for socialism Wesker
has, since she combines a care for humanity with caring for her
family. Wesker's socialist vision is based on a philosophy which
values the day-to-day care of people for each other (shown in the
attention to such activities as cooking, eating, working with wood),
and inevitably woman becomes central in this vision. Although
Wesker's belief in love and caring enables him to show men doing
unaccustomed tender things – Sarah's son Ronnie nurses his father
Harry after he has had a stroke – the basic sexual division of
labour in the family is not questioned. Both Sarah and her daughter
Ada speak of 'living out' socialism, but for both it means primarily
living it out as wife and mother – Sarah's involvement in anti-
fascist activity in the 1930s is real, but it is as a mother we see
her. And when Ada and her husband Dave try to live out a utopian
socialism in Norfolk based on William Morris's principles, it is
Dave who is the craftsman, Ada who backs him up. Even in *Roots*,
where the central character Beatie wins a painful struggle to think
and speak for herself (prefiguring some of the pride in self-articu-
lacy in later plays by women writers), she is still set apart from
Ronnie in that he is the one with the love of high culture and she
is the one whose earthy origins hold her back from culture. The
women in Wesker's plays are strong, fierce, even articulate – but
although they are the custodians of passionately held values, they
are not allowed to test them out in the world, independently of
men and the family.

Sarah herself is curiously ambiguous: she is a mixture of earth-
mother, Jewish matriarch and socialist-realist heroine. But although
she represents all the values of a 'caring socialism', in her own
family there is something implicitly sinister about her. Her husband
Harry has always been 'weak', for reasons we are never apprised
of, unable to be a 'real man' to her 'real woman'. He can never
keep jobs; he is feckless; she has kept the family together. As the
trilogy progresses he has heart attacks, ending up helpless and
utterly dependent – reverting to being a 'child' to Sarah's 'mother'.
It is as though Sarah expands to fill Harry's space as he becomes
smaller and more helpless. In the process she is also 'de-sexed', as
though she has to be pinned down at the centre of the family as
eternal mother/nurturer (nursing Harry long after her children have

left home) but deprived of any sexual being in order to carry more effectively the symbolic burden of the socialist message. It is an ironic touch, in the work of one of the few men playwrights tackling the 'softer' sides of male emotion. However, this ambiguity about women is the inevitable consequence of a socialist vision rooted in an unswerving view of the traditional family and an insufficiently questioned division of labour within it.

Conclusions

These plays show how an unease with the state of the family and sexual roles permeates many plays of the 1950s and 1960s. All the writers discussed here are aware of heterosexual tensions – Osborne using the terrors of a threatened virility to retreat from facing questions of new class allegiances in the affluent 1950s, Delaney exploring the resistance of women to conventional motherhood, Jellicoe criticising male sexual game-playing, and Wesker asserting a socialist vision through (in part) a defensive reassertion of family values. But even at this stage, with virtually no public presence of feminism, the women writers can see the issues of sexual politics marginally more clearly than their male counterparts. Since threats to definitions of 'virility' do not affect women personally, and since greater political and personal self-identity for women inevitably involves critiques of the conventional family, it is not surprising that for both Delaney and Jellicoe (very different though they are as writers) women characters are given positive space. Both their plays discussed here end with affirmations of birth – problematic but still affirmative. They both also show women as explicitly sexual beings. For the male writers female sexuality and birth are issues of anguish, since to see woman as sexually independent is bound to challenge notions of male dominance, and seeing women as mothers touches on the deeply-rooted ambiguities about woman as life-giver or castrator.

There are two very interesting ways in which these plays place women in their imaginative worlds, and these ways are in a sense pre-feminist. The first is that women are essentially confined to the conventionally feminine, to a secondary role, to dependence on men, and this is reflected both in the structure of the plays and in their content. Alison in *Look Back* and Greta in *The Knack* are contained by being defined only in relation to men. Alison, like Greta, is a threat when there is any suggestion of the female (i.e., the sexual) which is likely to threaten the men's concept of virility. Even though Jellicoe is far more satirical about the ritual sexual games which men play, her women do not break through, and have no significant contact with one another. Even with Wesker, whose Sarah is a powerful and politically very important figure, the de-sexed female still remains (with its strengths as well as its weaknesses, it must be admitted) contained within the feminine role. All the plays are fascinating precisely because they express in different ways some sense that the conventional masculine and feminine roles are under pressure. *A Taste of Honey*, however, is slightly different: here what is interesting is that the feminine is largely rejected for the female; the real emotional terms of reference in this play are between the women, and the strong sense of a female identity is shared between Helen and Jo. This, too, however, is fraught, since they do not so much choose one another as are forced together in a world where men fail them, or are sexually incomplete. *Taste* does not follow the other plays in assuming that women can only exist in relation to men; but it is like them in that the all-female option is ambiguous at best, and the best of a bad job at worst.

The questions which hover behind these plays spill over from heterosexuality into homosexuality – in the plays discussed subtextually, rather than explicitly. Explicit treatments of homosexuality reveal some of the same tussles – particularly since the best-known of these are by men. Later, in the 1960s, the subject was broached more clearly: in *The Killing of Sister George* by Frank Marcus (1965), in which crude lesbian stereotypes are used as a metaphor for media manipulation, and also to reaffirm by implication 'correct' definitions of femininity (George as the unnatural man, Childie as the thwarted mother); in John Osborne's *A Patriot for me* (1965, heavily censored) in which the misogyny is less important than the way Osborne deals directly with the political and ethical relationship between militarism, masculinity and male homosexuality; in Joe Orton's work in the 1960s, where sexual issues emerge from repression into earthy and shocking violence, still with a misogynist impetus. Written in a climate of stage censorship and before sexuality had been identified as having a political dimension, all these plays struggle to express imaginatively an issue which at the time had no name. Male playwrights in the 1970s, on the other hand, have written about women and sexuality in a very different climate, with the presence of feminism as one of the radical forces of their time.

10
Men playwrights in the 1970s

The legacy of Brecht

Brecht's *The Mother* (written in 1930–1 and based on the novel of the same name by Maxim Gorki, published in 1907), hitherto a comparatively little-known play in Britain, was performed a number of times in London and around England in the early 1970s. It is a play explicitly about a woman's relationship to the Communist movement in Russia between 1905 and 1917. At the beginning of the play Vlassova is hostile to politics, dislikes violence and worries over her son Pavel: is he well? Is he getting enough to eat? – conventional maternal concerns. As the play progresses, she is drawn into her son's struggles – learning to read, going on demonstrations, getting beaten up. By the end her entire life is taken up with campaigning out on the streets for peasants and workers to join in fighting against the Tsar and for Communism.

The Mother travels the longest possible road to full political consciousness – from being a backward individual she progresses to the most advanced kind of political leadership. But this journey is defined entirely in terms of the experience of the men; political struggle, for instance, is experienced solely at the workplace, and only includes women insofar as they are engaged in productive work outside the home. For the Mother to 'join' them she has to leave her own terrain – her home – and join the men on theirs. Inevitably this also means a rejection of the very female, caring qualities which made her so ripe for Brecht's conversion in the first place. Her concern for Pavel and his friends diminishes as she becomes politically active. Pavel complains with a wry pride that she isn't looking after him any more; and when Pavel is later killed even the Mother herself passes judgement on her female 'weakness': 'My weeping wasn't rational. But when I stopped, my stopping was rational.' (*The Mother*, translated by Steve Gooch, Eyre Methuen, 1978, p. 52.)

Vlassova actively destroys her femaleness (sexuality is not a problem since she is shown as old and therefore past it from the very beginning) in order to become a 'socialist'. The Mother remains a token, isolated woman in a world of men, with no choice but to accept their terms – the terms of the 'rational' class struggle of men at the expense of the 'irrational' private world of women. And yet this rejection is ironic, since the Mother's potency as a symbol of a radically altered consciousness exists precisely because she is vulnerable and caring. The implications of the way she, as a woman, is co-opted into the men's struggles are complex; on the one hand the economic and political issues that Brecht dramatises are gritty class issues. But his lack of awareness of the different ways in which men and women experience class oppression leads him to have an ironically divisive effect on his audience. The Mother is a cypher who validates the raising of class-consciousness for men; thus to the men in the audience she affirms the importance of something they already know about or have access to. But to the women in the audience she represents a 'real' message – leave home and follow your men, for that is where the class struggle is. Such a message can only be meaningful to other token women (those without home ties or those already there) or produce guilt and impotence in others.

The Mother was an explicit structural model for Red Ladder's play *Strike While the Iron is Hot* (later retitled *A Woman's Work Is Never Done*) (touring, 1974–6), but the group consciously decided to introduce overt sexual-political content. Thus, although their play was based on the model of the ordinary-wife-and-mother-becomes-militant-socialist, the balance was also redressed; husband Dave is actively challenged by wife Helen to share equally in housework and childcare as she becomes more involved in work and politics outside the home. The political struggle is located at home and at work, with the paradigm of an equal personal/political partnership replacing the woman-joins-the-men model of Brecht's play.

John McGrath

Brecht's play was also the acknowledged model for *Yobbo Nowt*, toured by the 7:84 Theatre Company during 1975–6. Marie sees herself (and is seen in a running chorus throughout the play, though with increasing irony) as a 'nobody'; the mother of two teenagers, and wife to a sexually brutal man who won't let her get a job. She kicks him out and embarks on a 'hobby' – finding out about capitalism – as well as building a new life with her children. Through her hobby she finds out all about the state, class exploitation, trade unionism, but nothing about sexism, feminism or sexuality – she decides not to bother with 'fellas' just yet. Her journey to self-determination includes tussling through her relationship with her children, including some witty scenes where her son has to express his macho pride even in something as small as making toast. Marie doesn't join anything, nor does she produce a correct class line – but she still acts as a tabula rasa on which can be inscribed lessons about politics, as defined by men. The play is full of vigour and wit – McGrath acknowledges the 'personal' insofar as Marie decides to live independently without her husband – but in the didactic scenes, where Marie is 'learning' about politics, sexual oppression is subsumed under a pre-existing definition of class exploitation, rather than bringing its own analysis with it to add to the traditional class analysis.

McGrath has expressed some suspicion of 'feminism' as a distinct response by women to their oppression:

> in my plays I have tried to expose the evils of sexism.
> However, I do not subscribe to the 'noble tractor driver' method of presenting workers, nor will I subscribe to the 'noble feminist' method of presenting women, workers or otherwise.
>
> (John McGrath, letter to *Time Out*, 29 April 1977)

It is hard to know what he means by the 'noble feminist', since such a figure does not really exist in either socialist or feminist writing, but the suspicion appears to stem from the assumption that the assertion of solidarity between women acts as somehow diversionary from the main class struggle – an accusation that was levelled at the Women's Liberation Movement in its early days.

Indeed, a suspicion that for McGrath feminism was merely a minor skirmish in the studies of middle-class women was confirmed by the very structure of an earlier play, *Trees in the Wind*, written in 1971. The play is set in a flat shared by three young, middle-class women. Little happens until the arrival of a working-class man, who galvanises the emotions of each woman in turn. The women have no visibly significant relationships with each other, and only spark into dramatic conflict when the man operates their emotional puppet strings. McGrath puts some extraordinary speeches into the women's mouths – violence in Vietnam, an account of sexual turmoil which one woman is going through – but they are dramatically isolated from one another in their separate rooms and emotionally paralysed unless activated by a man.

In *Little Red Hen* (1975) the eponymous heroine, a granny, narrates and creates a moral tale about the Scottish Labour Party to her young, innocent grand-daughter. It is almost as if Brecht's *Mother* had returned to pass the same kind of message on. In *Blood Red Roses* (1980), however, there is an interesting shift, in that a feminist consciousness in which a woman is concerned about her personal development and her sexuality, is shown as much more compatible with the old-style class consciousness, as defined by the men.

Portable Theatre and sexuality

Portable Theatre, founded in 1968 by Cambridge graduates David Hare and Tony Bicât, was for a brief while a genuine touring writers' theatre, run by a generation of new 'angry' young men. Portable's plays lashed out at the falseness of the 'culinary', consumerist theatre, experimenting with epic, didactic, surrealist forms and, after the abolition of state censorship, including a franker treatment of sexuality.

Lay By (1971) was one of the rare successful examples of a collaboratively-written play, by seven male writers who have since taken very different paths: Howard Brenton, Brian Clark, Trevor Griffiths, David Hare, Stephen Poliakoff, Hugh Stoddart and Snoo Wilson. The play was based on a case of rape and indecent assault; Jack, a van driver, assaults Lesley, a young junkie, with the aid of his consort Marge. The play is spare and makes cinematic leaps backwards and forwards in time and space (exploiting the new free approach to staging in touring theatre) and ends with two hospital orderlies (male) officiating at the deaths of the trio. It is a harsh, macabre piece, using pornography and sexual exploitation as a metaphor for the exploitation of the media and the power of the false images of the dominant culture. Sex and/or violence motivate the actions of every character – except perhaps Lesley, the rape victim. Women are shown to be victims of male sexual violence, but at the same time the sex and violence in the writing itself often comes dangerously close to being simply titillatory, a reproduction of the very phenomena it seeks to expose.

In part this is due to the fact that the terms of the critique are male defined – within the play women, the most oppressed, are either victims (Lesley) or supportive of the men (Marge). The women themselves do not rebel, and the power of the play as a shock tactic, to make us look at the violence around us, is muted and partial because it remains within the control of men.

David Hare

David Hare has developed something of a reputation for writing about women in theatre and television. More than almost any other male playwright (apart, perhaps from Howard Brenton) he is seen as an Osborne-like figure, speaking for the post-post-war generation of radical young men driven to anger and anguish by the time of change we are all living through. He has described himself as a writer of 'history plays' and 'love stories', concerned to show 'the extraordinary intensity of people's personal despair' (*Sunday Times* colour supplement, 26 November 1978).

In the same article he attempted a theoretical rationale for the function of theatre:

> Judgement is at the heart of the theatre. A man steps forward and informs the audience of his intention to lifelong fidelity to his wife, while his hand, even as he speaks, drifts at random to the body of another woman. *The most basic dramatic situation you can imagine*; the gap between what

he says he is and what we see him to be opens up, and in that
gap we see something that makes theatre unique; that it
exposes the difference between what a man says and what
he does. (my italics)

At the heart of his rationale is a vision of theatre as being about
the contradiction between words and action as they are defined
through the male experience. The metaphor in the above quotation
is not accidental, not universal, but specific to a conception of
theatre and history which conceives of active protagonists as male.
In the light of such a view, Hare's choice of women as apparently
central figures in his plays may appear contradictory – *Slag*
(Hampstead Theatre Club, 1970) *Teeth 'n Smiles* (Royal Court
Theatre, 1975) and *Plenty* (National Theatre, 1978) all have a
main woman character. His decision to write about women, claims
Hare, stems from:

> A sense of the waste of women's potential, the way they are
> patronised and not implicated in the mess that Westerners
> have made of their civilisation. Looking at the world through
> the eyes of women is to see the world more clearly.
>
> (Interview, *Time Out*, 7 April 1978)

In *Slag* Ann runs a small, failing, public school for girls. She is
assisted by Elise, so desperate for sex that she thinks herself into
an hysterical pregnancy. Joanne, at 23, seems to be intended as a
representative of the new feminist ideology. The play could have
been an apt satire on the empty rituals of upper-class education
were it not for the fact that most of the wit and jokes are at the
expense of female physiology and sexuality – and through the three
women Hare constructs a montage of frigid, authoritarian, petty,
man-hating nymphomania. The play thus becomes a tirade against
women and against feminism – a feminism which Hare has in any
case misrepresented (whether deliberately or not), since he makes
no distinction between radical and socialist feminism. Given the
hostility of the media to the Women's Liberation Movement in
1971 it is perhaps not surprising that Hare should similarly have
pilloried what he took to be a fascinating but dangerous phenomenon, but it sets a somewhat ambiguous precedent for his later
putative interest in women.

Maggie, at the centre of *Teeth 'n Smiles*, is wild, ravaged, the dipso singer in a second-rate pop group doing its last gig at a Cambridge May ball. She destroys indiscriminately – herself, her singing, other people's singing, and in particular Arthur, her song-writer ex-lover. Maggie is sexy and charismatic, a kind of voluptuous chameleon, changing her identity according to what is demanded of her. By the end Maggie collapses, not knowing what she wants and certainly not having the stamina to make a decision and act it out. Her helplessness makes her into a victim, a sacrifice on the altar of personal pain and the demands of the artistic experience; a post-Romantic artist who suffers for the cause of a truthful and painful vision – but even here she is not allowed artistic autonomy by her author. She does not survive, while Arthur does. He, immaculate in his white suit, is the real creative artist, while Maggie, the interpretative female, a token woman in a man's world, cannot 'be' a man, and therefore cannot survive alone.

Susan, in *Plenty*, is cool and upper class. During the war she was a courier in the Resistance, a responsible individual. That moment of independent glory was brief. Her life after the war is a series of stepping stones, through loneliness, by way of a ruthlessly calculated (and failed) effort to persuade a working-class man to get her pregnant, to eventual insanity. For David Hare women are essentially innocent bystanders to the main events of history, powerless to influence them, and rarely responsible individuals. Inevitably they must fail if they try to be independent and survive in a man's world, or they will become ciphers (as romantic victims) of a view of male despair.

Conclusions

There have been very few plays by men (socialists or liberal radicals) in the 1970s about women, set on female social territory. Two exceptions were *Female Transport* by Steve Gooch (Half Moon Theatre, 1973) about women on a convict ship, and *Touched* by Stephen Lowe (Nottingham Playhouse, 1978; Royal Court Theatre, 1981) about a group of Nottingham women at the end of the Second World War. There have been genuine attempts by many men to write differently about women – challenged by

feminists they have become aware of the unthinking female stereotypes – dolly bird, nagging wife, ageing harridan – and have taken
that criticism seriously. So far their responses have been partial: to
write larger roles for actresses, or to place a single token woman
at the apparent centre of a play (i.e., as 'heroine') does not necessarily mean the same thing as writing about women sympathetically
or with understanding.

In the above plays and many others women become either the
conscience of humanity (ripe for conversion to socialist consciousness) or the victim (emblem) of the oppression of Everyman (sic).
Either way the perspective still remains male-determined, and
women remain innocent, outside power relations, and either
asexual or sexually voracious. What is interesting is that these
plays simply represent variants on the 'feminine', in that the women
are either represented as innocents, who need to be instructed by
men (i.e., dependent on men for definitions of knowledge and
politics), or where they attempt to enter the sphere of the female
– i.e., to be independent and sexual, they must be imaginatively
isolated and 'punished'.

Where the radical male playwrights of the 1950s, perhaps uncon-
sciously, displaced political issues on to the sexual, the male playwrights of the 1970s cannot be so innocent. Certainly they are
beginning to re-examine their views of women, but so far they
have denied women sexuality, or contained that sexuality by
destroying the woman. Alternatively women are allowed access to
political power, but only if they follow the Brechtian model and
become one of the lads. Using woman as a metaphor may look
like a compliment, but it is an unconscious way of denying her a
real part of the stage action.

There are two ways of evaluating this: the first is to say that
men, despite some of their best intentions, are still unable to
'imagine' women clearly, without the taint of their own misogyny
and conditioning. But if we approach the misogynistic treatment
from a slightly different point of view, we have what I believe is a
more illuminating conclusion. If we see the misogyny as the largely
inevitable consequence of the fact that each writer approaches the
world through their particular gender-biased imagination, then one
is faced with different insights into the ways in which men depend
on misogyny to give much of their work symbolic point. Using

women as metaphor may produce stage imagery of emotional reverberance, but it can no longer be the innocent thing of the 1950s, since feminism is now able to expose what is going on.

It seems to me that the really interesting work from men writers, in direct or indirect response to feminism, is where they explore male-male relations in new ways – in other words, when they are as explicit about their gender bias as many women writers are about theirs. Perhaps not surprisingly this has come most clearly from gay male writers – such as Noel Greig and Drew Griffiths, whose work has already been discussed, and in the better-known play *Bent* by Martin Sherman (Royal Court, 1979), an extraordinarily powerful and moving play about the Nazis and Jewish and homosexual persecution. The play explores a complex of emotional and political stances in the way it follows one man and his tactics for survival not just in a world hostile to his homosexuality, but against the opposition of homicidal, homophobic Nazism, in which the dilemmas of loyalty and betrayal are painfully ranged. There are also two very powerful scenes in which two men 'make love' simply by using words, and neither looking at one another nor touching one another – scenes which are both erotic in their linguistic effect, but also poignantly expressive of love which is forbidden and punishable, and yet still has to find ways to express itself.

Another play, in a very different sexual mould, is *Operation Badapple* (Royal Court, 1983) by G. F. Newman. This is a play, also with an all-male cast, about police corruption. Through the encounters of a rural police group with a metropolitan police group, the intricacies of police corruption are revealed; the power in the play lies in the care of its plotting, in which different levels of corruption (from petty to grand) are gradually revealed, but from a gender point of view, in the ways that male-male power games operate. Whenever any male character is emotionally at bay, when his position of power is under threat or actually being undermined, he resorts to the use of sexual swear-words; the term 'fucking cunt' appears at such moments, but because the term is applied only to other men, the play is a very good example of the way (a) heterosexuality and (b) women represent simultaneously the most intense and the most despised aspects of these men's psyches. Here again it is very important indeed not simply to dismiss the expressions of misogyny simply as hatred of women. They are certainly that, but they are also comments on the way the men need to displace their own emotional frustrations on to expletives in which the 'bad' is represented by female heterosexuality.

Although the configurations are different, and the plays of the 1970s deal more openly with social and political issues than the plays of the 1950s and 1960s, most of the plays by male play-wrights still define women either by containing them as the femi-nine, or, if they enter the female sexual arena, by imaginatively 'punishing' them. This applies even in cases where women are apparently being given the accolade of being political activists, or involved in the political arena. The function of women in two plays, both first produced in 1983, highlights the way in which the concept of the feminine actually blocks the male imagination from actually realising the implications of the feminist. In both *The Genius* by Howard Brenton, and *Maydays* by David Edgar, women appear to be written and taken seriously. In the first Gilly is a brilliant mathematician and inventor. She is a student, lower in status than Leo, who is a professor of mathematics. Intellectually, then, we are meant to think of them as 'equals'. However, in the course of the play, Leo is represented as actively sexual, and also as the man with a conscience about leaking secrets. Gilly is the non-sexual feminine with a brain – a curious kind of anomaly. In *Maydays* there is no spurious 'equality' offered; the play is explicitly the story of its central, male figure, Martin. Both plays (perhaps by coincidence) end with a kind of apocalyptic scene at Greenham Common; these scenes are complex, but both imply similar messages, and work off similar clusters of aesthetic symbolism. The Greenham scenes are presented to us in both plays courtesy of the women characters, Gilly and Amanda. But despite Gilly's 'genius' in mathematics, and despite Amanda's periodic presence as one of the women on the left, the central dilemmas of the plays – and very fascinating they are too – have been conveyed to us via the men. The women are asexual, unpolitical (Gilly), or coolly abstract about sex, politically volatile (Amanda) and neither is ever really seen in control of any dilemma or serious self-doubt. In terms of the weight of each play, the women are powerless, relatively simple as characters, and politically totally ineffective.

And yet part of the aesthetic power of the final Greenham scenes is meant to be the contrast between the 'feminine' softness of women and the 'masculine' hardness of nuclear weapons. This has the meaning of a poignant fight against aggression; but since the plays have demonstrated the relative political passivity of the women, the final scenes must be quite meaningless, since power is not being met with power. There is then a profound ambiguity in these final scenes: if they are meant to convey hope through protest, then it must be a futile hope. The women cannot carry the meaning of strength. If, however, the playwrights intended these scenes to be cynical demonstrations of the futility of political action, then that too will be demonstrated via the powerlessness of the demonstrators – the women. Either way, the women are only cyphers in the arena of the political, which is still defined according to the presence and the concerns of men. It is a curious kind of chivalry which appears to be giving women the credit to lead political change, while at the same time demonstrating that women are not even at first base in the political arena.

11

The fourth phase: women playwrights in the 1970s and early 1980s

Pam Gems

Pam Gems was born in 1925 and spent her early life in a small village in the New Forest. After the Second World War she went to Manchester University to study psychology, and married in 1949. Between 1952 and 1965 she had four children, and during the 1950s and 1960s she wrote plays for radio and television, some of which were produced. In 1970 she moved to London with her family and began writing for fringe theatre. An autobiographical entertainment called *Betty's Wonderful Christmas* was produced at the Cockpit Theatre in the winter of 1972–3. She was then invited to write some 'sexy pieces' for the Almost Free Theatre, and responded with two monologues – *My Warren*, about a woman living alone in a bed-sitter, and *After Birthday* about a working-glass girl who has just aborted – which were put on in the spring of 1973 preceding the Women's Theatre Season, for which she wrote *Miz Venus. . . .* She also worked on both the productions done by the Women's Company – writing *Go West, Young Woman* in 1974 and translating Marianne Auricoste's *My Name is Rosa Luxemburg* in 1976.

During 1974 she began work on *Queen Christina*,[1] which was later turned down by the two male directors at London's Royal Court Theatre:

> They said it was too sprawly, too expensive to do and anyway, it would appeal more to women. That got to me.

> I mean, would they ever have said 'We can't do this play, it will appeal to men'?
>
> (Interview with the author, *Spare Rib*, September 1977)

Many theatres will accept plays which need rewriting, but the comment reported by Pam Gems is explicit in its hostility to women as 'subject matter'; her experience with *Queen Christina* has many echoes in the experiences of other women playwrights. The play was subsequently produced at The Other Place, the RSC's studio theatre in Stratford, in 1977, the first play by a woman to be done there. In 1976 *Dead Fish* was produced at the Edinburgh Festival, and the following year was given a new production at the Hampstead Theatre Club under the title of *Dusa, Fish, Stas and Vi*;[2] it then transferred to the Mayfair Theatre for a West End run. *Piaf*[3] was first produced at The Other Place in 1978, transferred to the Warehouse, the RSC's London studio theatre in 1979, and then to the Piccadilly theatre in the West End in 1980.

Pam Gems is an important writer for a number of reasons; she spans the experiences of two generations; she lived through the war as an adult, yet she has an openness to present-day ideas. She writes boldly about women – reappraising mythologised heroines such as Piaf and Christina, and her work has been both successful and 'popular' within the enclave of 'new' serious writing. She engaged with the early developments in feminist theatre, from which she later withdrew:

> I think the phrase 'feminist writer' is absolutely meaningless because it implies polemic, and polemic is about changing things in a direct political way. Drama is subversive.
>
> (Interview with Ann McFerran, *Time Out*, 21–7 October 1977)

Although for her the distinction between 'political' change and the effect of theatre has made her reluctant on occasions to identify herself as a feminist writer, her grasp of the dilemmas of being female and heterosexual, coupled with her approach to class, makes her work provocative and important. A theme which runs through most of her plays is the way individual women develop and sustain their tactics for survival. In particular, she is gripped by the qualities of female survival at the bottom of the social heap.

Piaf is so far the clearest expression of faith in women's basic resilience. Pam Gems does not show us the sparrow Piaf, to be patronised in her journey from street-urchin to mythologised success. She shows a Piaf who is vulnerable to the values and pressures of her chosen milieu – drink, drugs, sexual patronage – but who continually bounces back. Piaf and her friend Toine are tough street-women; they swear, Piaf pisses onstage (no coyness, no feminine lace curtains over gutter survival), and the women's friendship survives the succession of men who pass through their lives. Piaf is a woman for whom independence and success lead to sexual freedom and personal autonomy – as if she were a man. But she never loses the spiky values of her childhood, suspicious of the seductive demands of showbiz, and refusing to abandon her loyalty to her class origins: 'I'm not bloody joining and there's an end to it. You think being born working-class is like having a disease.' (*Piaf*, Amber Lane Press, 1979, p. 96.)

Pam Gems' Piaf is a woman for whom female independence means an active and vigorous sexuality, which at its most intense parallels the orgasmic satisfaction she gets from singing, and a bristly, individualistic identification with being working class which enables her to resist all the flannel and hypocrisy of showbiz.

A consequence of her admiration of the working-class qualities of survival is Pam Gems' ambiguity towards middle-class women, especially those who espouse pro-working-class politics. She acerbically satirised the trendy left in *The Project* (a lunchtime production at the Soho Poly, London, in 1976, later expanded and retitled *Loving Women*) and more seriously explored it in the successful *Dusa, Fish, Stas and Vi*. Four women are together in a London flat: Stas, a physiotherapist whoring on the side to save up the money to study marine biology; Vi, a faddist who goes from anorexia to mysticism; Dusa, separated from her husband who in the course of the play runs off with their children; and Fish, owner of the flat (courtesy of Daddy), an earnestly committed socialist. Each woman reaches a watershed in her life. Stas finally saves enough money to go off to Hawaii; Vi recovers enough to take a job as a traffic warden; Dusa's children are retrieved; but Fish, whose lover has left her for another woman, commits suicide. Where the three others come through their crisis with renewed strength, Fish goes under – her socialist fervour providing no defence against her inability to cope with life without her man.

The play treats Fish's dilemma poignantly when she is torn between trying to feel differently and trapped in jealousy and loneliness; but in setting her apart from the others as the only 'politico' and in bringing her to suicide, there is an implicit judgement that political commitment either blocks people from coping with their emotions, or makes them even more vulnerable to their own moralism; they try piously to change the world on behalf of the working class but can't even get their own lives together. Matters are compounded by the fact that as far as one can tell Fish is not a feminist and therefore has no theory other than her mechanistic socialism to fall back on. The play asserts the dilemmas without exploring them. It appears that Fish's middle-class origins condemn her as a woman, making it impossible for her to find solidarity with other women – something which perhaps speaks of Pam Gems' suspicion of 'middle-class' feminism simply because it is 'middle-class' in its origins.

Queen Christina, however, hooks directly and fascinatingly into many of today's most original feminist concerns – initiated by women whose class origins are very similar to those of the tragic Fish. The play is a sprawling epic, spanning half the seventeenth century. Christina is a kind of Renaissance woman, brought up as a boy in order to be groomed for the Swedish throne in the absence of a male heir. She hunts, fights, is bi-sexual and takes an active part in military and political decisions. Her first crisis occurs when the court, again worrying about the succession, begins to put pressure on her to marry and produce a male heir. From being brought up to 'behave like a man', she is suddenly being forced to 'behave like a woman'. She abdicates and travels round Europe, trying to find another way of life. She is repelled by French bluestocking women who affect to despise men; finally she settles in Italy with a male lover. Her second major crisis is when she realises that her lover, like everyone else in her past, has been using her for her status. She colludes in a plot to kill him, but afterwards recoils from what she has done, realising that she hates killing and is 'not a man'. As she ages she discovers a love for female things – like baking and the 'smell of babies'. Her last major act is to help young Italian republicans escape from their persecutors. She

dies, having experienced the ultimate benefits of ruling-class privilege, having known political and sexual power as both a man and
a woman but having left the choice of motherhood until it is too
late.

Pam Gems has described *Christina* as a 'uterine' play; and the
play's action, centring on the existential choices facing Christina,
faces us with the same questions that political feminism has
explored in theory and political analysis; what is it to be 'male'?
What is it to be 'female'? Pam Gems uses Christina's class to
highlight the question: since she has been able to live as both man
and woman, has that given her more freedom or less? There is
ultimately one deprivation she regrets: motherhood. It is as though
the play's final question is whether a woman can live fully without
having been a mother; and although *Christina* does not provide a
simple answer, it is a question which virtually no other play by a
woman has explored with such poise. Despite the play's unwieldy
structure, Christina's central experience gives it a core of great
power, playing out the possible options between – as the play puts
it – 'the flesh and circumstances'. The play joins a small number
of other writings which have investigated the conundrum of being
born into one sex and living as another – Virginia Woolf's *Orlando*
(a novel, published in 1928) dealt with a similar theme through
fantasy; *Christina* asks explicit social questions about the relationship between the destinies of class and/or biology, and it will be
interesting to see whether Pam Gems develops the theme further.

Pam Gems' work so far shows a definition of 'femaleness' which
is fierce in its claims for sexual autonomy and (less explicitly, but
just as tenaciously) for motherhood. Her work is strongly women-
centred, in that men come and go in the plays, and none of her
major female characters are seen working through relationships
with men. This gives her the freedom to explore relationships
between women, their wit and friendship, their individual solidarities. She has not so far written about women as political activists
– except where their humane sympathies are touched; this stems
from a suspicion of organised politics (socialist or feminist) and
from a concern which is one of her great strengths – the quest to
discover how far social/sexual behaviour is biologically determined.
She is also interested in the 'ordinary' dimensions of heroic or

mythic women, in how they combine the psycho-sexual demands of being female with being leaders or idols.

In evaluating the influences of the feminisms on Pam Gems' work, we have a fascinating mixture: in *Piaf* and *Dusa* there is a very clear radical feminist dynamic operating in the way that the friendships and interdependencies between the women exist absolutely in their own right, and are given strong and continuous stage space (*Dusa* has an all-women cast). At the same time, both these plays and *Christina* show great need for, and dependence on, men. Indeed, for both Piaf and Fish dependence on men is a despairing thing, since each looks for happiness with a man and yet neither finds it, showing something of a bourgeois feminist dynamic. Christina, on the other hand, is less concerned about men than the loss of motherhood; for her the radical feminist principle of sexual self-determination (something demonstrated beautifully in *Piaf*) has led to her undervaluing motherhood until it is too late. For Dusa, however, motherhood is central, and her story line is entirely about getting her children back from her husband who has 'stolen' them.

All the women in these plays are powerfully and confidently sexually self-determining; they all also, within their defined spheres, demonstrate the bourgeois feminist dynamic of individual existential power over their lives. However, at the same time, only the doomed Fish really tries to step outside the boundaries of what it can be to be female. The plays thus interweave elements from both the radical and the bourgeois feminist dynamics, and the socialist feminist dynamic has little place – although Piaf carries with her the gritty values of her early street life, it is a lumpen, rather than a socialist quality. Piaf's attractive and effective anarchy is echoed in a very different kind of play, *Aunt Mary*[4] (1982), in which a group of men – gay, transvestite, writers – live out a moving, surreal alternative lifestyle in which life and art are celebrated through style. It is a witty, almost camp play, in which Pam Gems continues her fascination with gender roles through the ways men create their lifestyles.

Caryl Churchill

Caryl Churchill went to Oxford University in the second half of the 1950s, where she wrote for student theatre. She married and had three children soon after leaving, and during the 1960s wrote a number of radio plays. Her first stage play was *Owners*, produced at the Royal Court Theatre in 1972. Then came *Objections to Sex and Violence*, also staged at the Royal Court in 1975. Two plays in 1976 involved collaborating with two touring companies – *Light Shining in Buckinghamshire* (for Joint Stock), and *Vinegar Tom* (for Monstrous Regiment). In 1977 *Traps* was produced at the Royal Court, and she collaborated again with Joint Stock on *Cloud Nine*, which toured during 1979 before playing at the Royal Court and being revived there in a new production in 1980.

Caryl Churchill was closely associated with the Royal Court during the 1970s, and her writing career, like that of a number of other women playwrights, moved from the relative privacy of writing for radio from home, while her children were small, to coming out into the more public world of theatre as they grew up. This has also expanded her political horizons, particularly through the writing she has done with theatre companies.

> for years I thought of myself as a writer before I thought of myself as a woman, but recently I've found that as I go out more into situations which involve women, what I feel is quite strongly a feminist position and that inevitably comes into what I write. However, that's quite different from somebody who is a feminist using writing to advance that position.
>
> (Interview with Ann McFerran, *Time Out*, 21–7 October 1977)

Owners concerns a network of personal/property relationships, fanning down from the central figure of Marion, a successful property developer. Her husband Clegg is a butcher. Marion evicts a young couple from one of her houses, and ruthlessly cons them into letting her adopt their baby, since she and Clegg are unable to have their own. Clegg loses his shop, and possessing no real estate, having no control over Marion, and unable to produce a child, he puts most of his energies into plotting various ineffectual attempts to murder Marion, while Marion's assistant keeps trying to commit suicide.

It is a strange play; redolent with imagery of death, disintegrating flesh and destruction, it presents a world of essentially isolated, 'alienated' individuals whose only satisfaction is to seek economic or psychological power over others or else unleash their violence upon themselves. Certainly the central character is a woman, but she is a woman whom power has de-sexed, and who in her turn emasculates her husband and violates everyone else. The play is murky in its implications as well as its imagery and its action; it portrays a clear pecking order based on the reduction of all values to those of property, but its treatment of Marion is at one level rather worrying, in that she appears to validate male fears of female sexual power. In this representation of the power of women, the play recalls Ann Jellicoe's ambiguity about Greta in *The Sport of My Mad Mother*, a sexual figure of great power, awaited and feared by the men. But Marion here is also sterile – echoing the way some of the male playwrights of the 1950s and 1960s had to 'deprive' women of part of their sexual and reproductive power.

It is as though women, given their head, and given the chance to act out society's values, will indeed turn out to contain a massive threat which they themselves cannot control. In some ways it is a tribute to the potential of female power, with Marion's aggression seen as a response to her own childlessness, her non-fulfilment 'as a woman'. It is an ambiguous and bleak play, in which the feminine dynamic is subverted by giving Marion social and economic power; but the power which she is given is a class power, the power of ownership, and this, in a sense, makes her into a 'man', emasculating her husband until all he can do is dream of killing her. Certainly it is a very powerful play, but one in which a simple socialist class analysis gives the chief impetus, with a bourgeois feminist dynamic permeated with irony in the character of Marion.

One of the main themes in *Objections to Sex and Violence* is the relationship between political terrorism and psychological violence. It is particularly evocative in the central relationship between two sisters, one settled in suburbia, the other on the run from the police. The 'political' dimension – the arguments for and against urban terrorism – are schematic and not integrated fully with the rest of the play, but there is also a tautly drawn portrait of an older Mary Whitehouse-type couple, bastions of respectable morality, but seething with repressed sexual fantasies.

In *Light Shining in Buckinghamshire*, Caryl Churchill tackled a historical subject: the spiritual and revolutionary fervour which gripped groups of people during the economic and social upheavals of England in the seventeenth century. While it lasted this fervour offered a utopian vision of economic and sexual freedom, with moments of literally ecstatic experience. The play includes a fair amount of contemporary documentary material, including an edited version of the Putney debates, in which the merits of freedom, democracy, common property and religious experience were argued, personally and philosophically. The experiences of women are given space in the play, and the approach to its subject matter combined a socialist with a feminist dynamic.

Vinegar Tom, written in the same year, draws on the same area of source material as *Light Shining*. As already mentioned in the section on Monstrous Regiment, it explores the web of fear, superstition and ignorance which provoked the witch-hunts of women in the seventeenth century. Being written for a female-dominated company, it shows only the way women were hunted as witches (not looking at witchcraft as something which men were accused of), because of the fear of female sexuality which was seen as evil and coming from the devil.

The play does, however, show how fear and superstition affected ordinary men as well as women, demonstrating the vulnerability of male sexuality; and one of the witch-hunters is assisted by a female accomplice. Class differences are also shown in the way that a middle-class woman suspected of being a witch would be seen as mad, while a peasant outsider woman would be seen as evil and burned. Both class and gender elements contribute to the way the story itself reveals aspects of a socialist-feminist dynamic. However, the play also included songs, sung by the cast out of character and in modern dress, in a kind of Brechtian alienation device, straight at the audience. All the songs contain a simple radical feminist message, of the ways in which men are to blame for seeing women merely as sex objects. The play thus contains within itself two different feminist dynamics, one in the dramatic, narrative form, the other in the song form. Because there is such a clear division between the dynamics, the audience is approached in two ways: first, as a united whole, where men and women can respond to the story, and secondly, the men are isolated from the women in that the songs carry an aggressive challenge to them. The difficulty, it has seemed to me, is that the complexity of the narrative is undermined by the crudeness of the songs. The narrative indicates very clearly where men are responsible, but it does so in a context which makes class and gender sense. The songs simply imply that all men are to blame and the two messages actually contradict one another.

Her next 'solo' play, *Traps*, was set in a country cottage, among a group of people in their late twenties/early thirties. One woman is regularly beaten up by her husband; one man has been in a mental hospital for raping and killing a woman; another woman is in a quandary because she can't decide whether or not to have a child. Sections of the action are replayed, characters change their relationships with each other within the stage 'reality' and the play ends in a moment of wistful togetherness, in which each character in turn bathes in the cottage's communal tin bath (in the same water). For the moment the group shares a reality – which they cannot achieve the rest of the time because they are 'trapped' in their own heads, and in a social reality which shifts like mercury and cannot be grasped. In her introduction to the published text Caryl Churchill explained her view of the play:

> it is like an impossible object, or a painting by Escher, where the objects can exist like that on paper, but would be impossible in life. In the play, the time, the place, the characters' motives and relationships cannot all be reconciled – they can happen on stage, but there is no other reality for them. . . . The characters can be thought of as living many of their possibilities at once. There is no flashback, no fantasy, everything that happens is real and solid as everything else within the play.
>
> (*Traps*, Pluto Press, 1978)

The comment indicates two of her continuing preoccupations: the flexibility inherent in the experience of stage reality as self-consciously illusory, and the basic philosophical question of how we perceive 'reality' and how we decide what is and is not 'real'. Translated into a political dimension – i.e., into a philosophy which accepts certain phenomena as material realities and therefore accepts that they can be changed, her position is more ambiguous. The link between *Traps* and *Light Shining* is clear; the vision of an ideal reality (a 'better society') is contained within a shifting set of definitions of reality in *Traps,* and in *Light Shining* it is contained within the visionary utopias of the seventeenth century. There is an equivocal attitude to change in this world view which is also present in *Cloud Nine.*

Act One is set in Victorian, colonial Africa, where paterfamilias Clive heads a family of three generations in which the values of authoritarian British imperialism are clearly linked with the repressive heterosexual values of family life. In a fast-moving, satirical series of set pieces Caryl Churchill reveals the complexity of sexual desire festering beneath the neatly pressed exteriors. The double standard rages; female and children's sexuality is denied; male homosexuality lurks, furtive and guilty. Act Two leaps a hundred years in historical time, but the characters are only twenty-five years older than in Act One. The second half is a collage of new lifestyles in London in the 1970s – an older woman learning to manage alone and discovering sexual pleasure for herself; a brother and sister living communally and bi-sexually with a mother and child. In the 'historical' half, imperialist and sexual values parallel each other, with a clear cause and effect; in the 'contemporary' half things have somehow changed, become more liberalised. The ways in which the individuals deal with their lives are sharp and moving, but there is no solid political dimension to the experiences, no cause and effect as there is in the first half, in other words, no political analysis and therefore no link between cause and effect. Sexual taboos about lesbianism, libertarian lifestyles are broken in that they are displayed onstage but they appear as an almost utopian moment – like an extended version of the last scene in *Traps*

The speed and wit of the first half structurally reinforce the socialist-feminist dynamic of the interconnection between class and gender. In the second half the libertarian lifestyles demonstrate the radical feminist dynamic of women determining their own sexuality and ways of living. But the second half lacks any sense of class (and socialist) dynamic, and the atomised structure reinforces this partial political disintegration. The relationship between the two halves is thus up for question. It could be argued that the second half is 'deliberately' open-ended, and will push the audience to come to its own conclusions. Possibly some members of audiences will do just this. But the two halves do have a formal relationship, in the continuity between characters, and this implies thematic continuity. The different styles of the two halves seem to be making a comment on the nature of history, and to be suggesting that we can put the past into order (neat, theatrical form) and analyse it in terms of both class and gender cause and effect, but that we cannot do the same with the present. Thus the radical feminist and bourgeois feminist dynamic which shows women in existential control of their lives both demonstrates the strengths of the feminist dynamic and undermines, by refusing, any kind of socialist dynamic. Depending on one's point of view, this means that the play is either open to any interpretation, or draws back from seeing the implications of its own hypotheses.

Top Girls (Royal Court, 1982) achieved success both in London and in New York. Most of Act One consists of a scene in which Marlene, recently promoted head of a secretarial employment agency, invites various women of distinction through history to a dinner party to celebrate. These women are taken from the Middle Ages to the nineteenth century, and include both real and mythical women. The scene intercuts accounts of these women's lives, with the speeches overlapping and interrupting one another, much in the way that 'real-life' conversations work. Each woman tells her life-story and each reveals herself to be a woman of complex achievements, successes and regrets. Between them they faced hardship, painful relationships with men, fraught motherhood – but none presents herself as victim; for each, taking responsibility for herself is the central thread. The remainder of the play consists of our seeing Marlene at work, seeing the other women in her office chatting to each other and interviewing prospective clients, and the intervention into Marlene's successful professional life of an illegitimate, slightly retarded daughter, who has been brought up by her sister Joyce. Angie, the daughter, comes to London because she adores Marlene and suspects that she is her true mother. In a sense the 'real' play ends here, with Angie arriving out of the blue, and we don't know how Marlene handles it. But sequentially, the final scene in the play which we see is a long, intense emotional scene between Marlene and her sister, living a life of isolation and some poverty somewhere out in the country. It is an extraordinary tour de force, echoing in a much tighter style, the divergences between sisters which figure in *Objections*.

Although the sisters have very different political ideas (Joyce is a socialist, Marlene a conservative), and have different lifestyles, each (like the women in the first scene) accepts entire existential responsibility for what she has done. Neither is visibly dependent on men. Marlene has been ambitious and successful; Joyce appears to be the opposite; but each has made her choice. In the light of this knowledge, while we may not know what Marlene decides to do about Angie, we have to assume that here too the decision will be calm and in Marlene's control. The fundamental dynamic, as it applies to all the women in the play, is the bourgeois feminist dynamic, coming through loud and clear and confidently. This does not mean that Marlene's 'success' is necessarily validated by the play; the play takes no moral or political attitude towards her, any more than it does towards Joyce. While we witness a stage peopled only by women, we do not witness any real adult relationships between the women which are more than contingent; but we do catch a glimpse of a close friendship between Angie and a schoolfriend, and we catch a glimpse of Marlene's murky past, in the person of a history (Angie and her own sister) which will not go away, and which at times intrudes. But it does not deflect Marlene. The fantasy element in the play, as well as the sleight-of-time manifested in the placing of the final scene, are formally interesting, but they do not alter the fundamental dynamic, which would be there still even if the first scene was cut, and the final scene put into its 'correct' time order.

In *Softcops* Caryl Churchill has an all-male cast, and the play is very literally a play of ideas in which the memoirs of two nineteenth-century criminals provide the peg on which to hang a witty and taut exploration of the attitudes of the state to authority and control and punishment. Violence and brutality are calculated, children initiated into the soft/hardcop routines. Everyone is drawn in to collude with the system of social control. The choice of an all-male cast possibly implies the suggestion that such state authority is 'male', but the play is not like *Operation Badapple*, and does not reveal the inner workings of a closed, all-male, social institution.

In that sense it is more about the way ideas on social control develop and change, rather than a realistic or satirical exposé of authority.

Mary O'Malley

One of the first real successes for women playwrights in the commercial theatre in the 1970s was Mary O'Malley's *Once a Catholic*. This started at the Royal Court Theatre in 1977, and later transferred to the West End. The play won awards from the London *Evening Standard* and *Plays and Players*, with Mary O'Malley considered the 'most promising' playwright of 1977. The play is set in a convent school in North London in the mid-1950s and juxtaposes the Catholic moralism of the nuns with the secular energy of the girls. It is a witty satire on Catholic sexual repressiveness, and mischievously tests the taboos of the commercial theatre with a packet of Tampax waved by a shocked nun, and a final act of 'sacrilege' when one of the girls affixes a long plasticine penis to a statue of Christ in church.

It is a clever and effective play; it rings the changes on that genre beloved of the English middle-class theatre – the boys' public school play, and in the course of following the fortunes of the girls in their O-level year, it makes a number of points. First of all, there is the contrast between the religious lessons of the nuns, their own sexual repression, and the sexual curiosity of the girls. The authoritarianism of the convent-school teaching is satirised; all the girls are called Mary, and the irony is that the one girl who is genuinely religious and who believes she has a vocation is actually the scapegoat for everything and is prevented from doing what she wants. The radical feminist dynamic is present here in the breaking of taboos (Tampax onstage) and in validating the girls' own subversive acts of rebellion. But in the process, the nuns are revealed merely as the voice of authority, and they are not given space as characters in their own individual right. The satire is gentle and ironic; interestingly, the two boys in the play have each found their own solution to their repressive schools, unlike the girls, who are far less confident. The active radical feminist dynamic which operates in presenting the world of the girls' school onstage, and in breaking various small taboos, is thus matched by a passive radical feminist element in which the young women's rebellion is contained by comparison to the young men's, and in which one woman is a continual victim, showing the central dilemma of the 'feminine'. The irony thus produced is in some ways all the more effective for this – adding a sad, almost tragic dimension to the play.

Nell Dunn

Steaming (1981) was Nell Dunn's first stage play. It began life at the Theatre Royal, Stratford, London, and then transferred to the West End, and has since been made into a film. It is set in the Turkish room of a public baths. Here a group of women, of various class backgrounds, meet regularly, once a week – a session which is important to them both for its physical and its psychological values. The single-set play takes place on the women's territory – no man is allowed in the room. Here we get to know the women, their life stories, their friendships. Violet runs the room, supplying tea, towels and understanding where necessary. There are two levels of dynamic which are worth analysing: the first is a very basic radical feminist dynamic which celebrates the detail and the variety of women's lives and emotions. From different backgrounds – moneyed middle-class to serious poverty – the women talk about their lives and try to become both clearer and more self-deter-mining. But this is simply the dynamic of detail. There is another dimension to the play which reveals a dynamic different from the radical feminist kind.

The baths are threatened with closure. The women decide, very much at the last moment, to organise a petition, and one of their number goes to make a speech at a council meeting. But the council takes no notice, and the closure is to go ahead. The last gesture of the women is to decide to occupy the baths, since that is all that is left to them. Leaving this last twist to one side for the moment (it comes quite spontaneously), the over-arching structure reveals that the very world we have witnessed, with its complex and varied lives, is now about to be destroyed because of the impersonal authority of the local council. This leaves the women in their traditional role – dependent for their very bricks and mortar, as well as their emotional support, on the say-so of others – the council are both men and women, but there is one sense in which this external authority is represented in the play as male. Although no men are allowed in the room (onstage), there is one man in the play. He only appears in silhouette, outside a frosted glass door. But he is very important and very powerful. He controls the 'system' – the heating, the hot water, the hardware which keeps the baths functioning for the women. He and Violet have a running battle, in which he is continually trying to sabotage her and, by implication, the rest of the women. So when the 'end' comes, we know that in a sense the enemy is already there in the baths. This actually serves to undermine the token gesture of resistance at the very end. The over-arching dynamic, then, is in fact the traditional, feminine dynamic, which is made all the more poignant because we have seen what strengths are going to be destroyed by the closure of the baths.

It could be argued that this feminine dynamic makes *Steaming* into a kind of morality play, which demonstrates to the audience how very precarious women's lives actually are. Perhaps. But for a production to have this effect it would have to look very carefully at the way the performances are to work. The women spend most of their time either nude or semi-nude. Given the traditional associations with the nude female body, the way it is objectified to the male gaze, to the complex and loaded erotic-sexual effect of nudity in performance, the play runs the risk (as indeed happened with its original production) of reinforcing the feminine dynamic through the relationship between the performers (feminine, naked and vulnerable) and the audience (male and female), who may be asked to take on the role of voyeurs. To do a production of this play is to have to confront and make decisions about the way the women performers present their bodies onstage; in a sense the audience, by 'eavesdropping' on the women's territory, is already in an outsider position. To reinforce that voyeurism is to reinforce the feminine dynamic at the expense of the radical feminist dynamic of detail.

Claire Luckham

Trafford Tanzi began life in Manchester in 1980; it then went, via Liverpool and the London fringe, to commercial success. Unusually, then, it comes from outside London, and this goes a long way to explaining the way it took hold of and subverted the popular working-class sport of wrestling. Its storyline recalls the simple agitprop lessons of the early 1970s feminist theatre work: the baby girl, brought up to be feminine and pretty and clean, resists and fights back, and is labelled a tomboy and told off by everyone, from her Mum to her teacher. Tanzi marries Dean, a wrestler, and at first, like a good wife, she supports him in his work, helps him train. During the course of so doing she becomes a wrestler herself, and begins winning titles in her own right; finally, she challenges Dean to a wrestling match, loser to do the housework. A little agitprop fable.

The wit of the play lies in the way the form and the content match; the story is told in a pastiche wrestling match – in ten rounds, each round one chapter in Tanzi's life story. However, the pastiche includes all the characters; everyone in the play has to be able to throw and be thrown, and the entire action is set in an actual wrestling ring, with lots of communication between performers and audience. At the end, the audience becomes the 'real' audience, and is incited (encouraged?) to cheer either for Tanzi or Dean – in other words, the audience is drawn into participation and into taking sides. Tanzi does in fact win the wrestling match, but Dean immediately calls for a rematch.

It is an exciting theatrical experience, but standing back a little, it is worth analysing the dynamics in some detail. The action takes place on territory normally controlled by men; there are some women wrestlers, of course, but in many places they are not allowed by law to wrestle, and there is a whole aspect of the idea of 'lady wrestlers' which evokes a semi-pornographic set of associations. Tanzi is shown to be able not only to do the job that men do, but – in this one instance – to do it better. Here we see a solid bourgeois feminist dynamic at work, in showing a woman taking a 'top' place on traditionally male-held territory. The bourgeois feminist dynamic is reinforced because Tanzi accepts the terms of the male-defined territory: housework is reckoned as work fit for the loser. Dean clearly accepts the fact that Tanzi has acquired a skill previously reserved to him, but there is no 'demand' on him to acquire the skill of housework because it is important work. He takes it as his 'punishment'. Obviously in the play this point is made with the passing wit of the contest, but only half the terms of the sex war have been altered, and the 'woman's' territory remains despised.

From a performance point of view, however, a radical feminist dynamic operates; in contrast to the traditional feminine persona onstage (cf. some of the dangers of *Steaming*) Tanzi, and all the other women in the play, have to be physically fit, athletic and agile. In its writing the play sends up traditional male and female stereotypes, and this gives it a running satirical edge which questions the demarcation of everyday gender roles. It is thus an interesting mixture of the bourgeois and the radical feminist, on the territory of working-class experience and popular cultural reference points, but it does not contain any socialist feminist dynamic as such.

Other women playwrights

The five playwrights whose work has been discussed have all made some kind of public impact with at least one play each. It is interesting to note that all of them have achieved their theatrical success at ages which are ten or more years older than their male counterparts. There are other older women playwrights, such as Olwen Wymark – and I suppose I must include myself in this too – and there is then quite an age gap between us, who perhaps did not become fully professional writers until our children were more or less grown up, and a very much younger generation of women playwrights, who have chosen to work in the theatre on the wave of confidence which feminism helped create in the 1970s. Many of these have begun writing in their twenties and bring a different set of assumptions and concerns into their work. Of course, there are still some older women who come to writing late – but there is certainly a discernible generation gap at the moment.

Some of the feminist-dynamic evaluations which have been applied to the plays in the previous chapter can be applied to the work of this 'younger' group, but the distinctions are by no means clear-cut. Certainly, from one point of view, the clearest is the taboo-breaking radical feminist dynamic, which introduces the hidden, the invisible, the 'private' and female, on to the public stage. Such subject matter is evident in the plays of Sue Townsend (e.g., *Womberang*, Soho Poly, 1979), set in a doctor's waiting room, written in sit-com style, with a subversive and anarchic comic touch. Her play *The Great Celestial Cow* (Joint Stock, 1984) is about Asian women, written in a semi-fairy tale style. Her work is easy, accessible, and places the female centre-stage in a style which owes much to the popularity of television naturalism and comedy.

Victoria Wood, who has already been mentioned as a performer, has also written plays, in which she too presents the female as material for the sympathetic absurd – in *Talent* (Sheffield Crucible Studio, 1978) there are jokes about menstruation and male virility. These tactics are very interesting because they reveal that there is a path from the radical feminist starting point to the 'female', which is entertaining, in the control of women, but does not seek to explore questions about gender or sex roles with any depth, or to suggest uncomfortable questions to the audience. What this work represents is the beginning of a presence by women, on their own chosen subject matter territory, in popular theatre. The intellectual and political content is minimal, but from the point of view of simple parity of representation of women onstage, this doesn't matter. It is only important when one begins to consider what the qualities are which make a play by a woman successful, and what is likely to happen to the genuinely radical, questioning work by women.

It seems that the winning, commercial and art-successful formula is some kind of combination of radical and bourgeois feminism. Out-front radical feminism on its own will not get very far, although bourgeois feminism will. A play such as *Daisy Pulls it off* by Denise Deegan (Southampton, 1983, later transferred to the West End) is a contemporary play about a girls' school, very much in the style of the Angela Brazil schoolgirl stories. Daisy wins a scholarship to the posh school, and despite being socially inferior, poorer, she finally wins through to being a moral heroine, a good sport, and with a concealed family fortune. This is really Cinderella stuff which uses the margins of the bourgeois feminist dynamic to show that if she is good and honest, a poor girl can reach the heights of social status and money – the upper-class feminine, in other words. What is interesting about many of the plays being written and produced in the early 1980s is the way in which they approach the 'female' as subject matter, or part of their subject matter, and whether, and to what extent, they either return to any of the feminist dynamics, or allow the 'female' to lead them back to the 'feminine'. The sit-com style is always bound to be ambiguous in this respect, unless it veers to the edges of farce and a kind of aesthetic subversion which cannot be ignored by the audience. *Daisy* is ultimately a very good Thatcherite play, in that Daisy is accepted, and accepts, a magical class mobility, which leaves her in the position of the rich, feminine young woman, presumably waiting for marriage. As a schoolgirl story, it is interesting to compare it to *Once a Catholic* in which the feminist dynamics are stronger and more questioning, while still keeping the comic edge.

The bourgeois feminist dynamic is very clearly evident in Louise Page's *Golden Girls* (RSC, 1984), which explores the pressures and challenges of athletics as they apply to a women's relay team. The play is very long, in short, staccato scenes, packed full of exposition and information about the way the athletics business, competition and drugs interweave. It pays very passing token lip service to the various personal pressures on the women, but despite the intriguing possibility of an ethical exploration of various issues, the play is consistent in the way it follows through the competitive instinct and the desire to 'win' in the women and the men. Each character makes his or her own decisions about what he or she is prepared to do to win – but the play is too sprawling and schematic to provide insight or dramatic tension. What is vindicated – despite the downbeat ending – is the desire to win above all; and this is the driving force behind the bourgeois feminist dynamic. Here the desire to explore the female produces the bourgeois feminist dynamic.

Another preoccupation in Louise Page's plays has been the mother-daughter relationship. In *Salonika* (Royal Court, 1982), the widow of a soldier killed in the First World War, returns with her daughter to the Greek beach where he died. There is a pleasingly surreal device whereby the dead man returns to speak to each of the characters, and during the course of the play the male characters touch on whether or not it is worth killing or dying in war. The mother-daughter relationship is shown to be irritable, frustrating to them both, but symbiotic. No man really succeeds in coming between them. In *Real Estate* (1984) a daughter leaves home, not to see her mother and stepfather for twenty years. She returns, pregnant, wanting to be reunited with her mother, who turns against her. Here too is a problematic, unresolved, mother-daughter relationship, counterpointed by two men – stepfather and lover – both of whom are desperate to have children to love, and who are seen in the play as the ones who do the domestic tasks of cooking together, and striking up real emotional rapport. The play is intriguing and ambiguous. Both mother and daughter are working women, tough and independent, competitive. The play suggests (perhaps inadvertently) some of the pitfalls of such role reversal; motherhood, it suggests, is incompatible, or at least deeply problematic, when it is combined with female independence. The suggestion that women transgress in rejecting the feminine (i.e., a particular version of motherhood) is reinforced by the stepfather's single (and simplistically presented) desire for fatherhood. In this the play recalls some of the problematic contained in Pam Gems' *Queen Christina* in which female independence is seen to be at the expense of motherhood.

This too is one of the elements in *Top Girls*, although here it is explored via the relationship between two sisters. These themes, of inter-familial relationships between women, are absolutely fascinating, and really only at the beginning of their time. The notion of 'sisterhood' encompassed by radical feminism has perhaps been translated by playwrights, who consider themselves as post-feminist, to mean sisterhood in the older sense, the sense of biological sisters, the sense of a female connection which is biological, unchosen, and which can very easily be the site of imaginative exploration.

Skirmishes by Catherine Hayes (1981) brought sisters and mother and daughters together in one room; a mother lies dying. The devoted(!) daughter has looked after her for years, and the other daughter arrives for a showdown. It is a raw play, in which the 'respectable' values of mother-daughter devotion and love and

sisterly affections are displayed, explored, ripped apart and tram-
pled on, with the constant, silent, threatening presence of the incon-
tinent, dying mother. It is a play of great taboo-breaking courage,
in which there can be no resolution, but in which the most private
secrets of the birth-death relationships become subject matter for
extraordinary, imaginative treatment. Here the territory is female,
both literally and emotionally. Another play which treated the
symbiotic mother-daughter relationship was '*Night Mother* by
Marsha Norman, first performed in America in 1983, and produced in London in 1985, in which a daughter announces one
Saturday evening that she intends to commit suicide. The play
covers the hours of that evening, and is similar to *Top Girls* in
its bourgeois feminist existential dynamic; it maintains a balance
through all the emotional events of the evening, in which the right
of each woman to choose is finally asserted, without any pretence
that pain can be avoided.

Elements in some of these plays approach a comprehension of
what can constitute tragedy in the lives of women – but a tragedy
which is unlike that of Antigone, whose dilemmas are all related
to the demands and deeds of men. These new plays suggest trag-
edies and conflicts for women which emerge from the condition of
being female, and which arise out of unresolved desires and
demands which women make on one another. That these have so
far been expressed in terms of family relationships is not at all
surprising; and it represents a widespread assimilation of the
radical feminist principle of reclaiming relationships between
women as important and fundamental.

Other kinds of taboos in representing the female appear in other
kinds of plays: *Like a Happy Ending* (Plymouth, 1979), by Val
McDermid, was a naturalistic, bittersweet story about a love affair
between a woman student and a woman counsellor; in *Find Me*
(1977) Olwen Wymark, an accomplished radio and stage drama-
tist, with an elliptical, semi-disquisitional style, explored the real-
life based story of a young woman diagnosed as 'mad'; the disintegration of self was represented literally with a number of actresses
playing the main character, sometimes simultaneously. In her next
play, *Loved* (1978), Amy, a woman in her middle years, decides
she has had enough of ministering to others, and looks for a more
independent future.

The other important new area in which women are slowly being represented in theatre is that of black women. In 1979 was the American production of Ntozake Shange's choreo-poem *For Colored Girls who have Considered Suicide When the Rainbow is Enuf*. It was put on at a large theatre, was bright, full of song and dance, immensely dynamic. Its all-female and all-black cast had tremendous success in New York, with black and white audiences. Here, however, it was both too soon and too foreign, I suspect. It did not do well. More indigenous black writing and performing have begun to surface since, however. Performer Joy Lemoine toured a one-woman fringe show during 1981; the Black Theatre Co-operative (with a white male director) put on a zappy production of *And All Things Nice*, by a young black woman, Carol Williams (1980), and Grace Dayley has written a stark, direct and naturalistic account of the impact of a young West Indian woman's pregnancy on her and her family in *Rose's Story*[5] (1983). The field is expanding rapidly.

It may be evident from the various discussions of plays throughout this book that there is no immediate, simple conclusion to be drawn about the theatrical forms which women choose. The opposite, in fact. The polemical, the comic, the naturalistic, the surreal, have all figured in the work of different women writers. There have been plays which appropriate verse and transform it – Melissa Murray's *Ophelia*, which was Shakespeare's *Hamlet* turned on its head, where Ophelia falls in love with her maid, and in which prose and poetry were interwoven; there have been plays which have translated the idea of the women's 'consciousness-raising group' into the traditional form of the one-set play – *Steaming* does that, and so did Cherry Potter's *Audience* (Common Stock, 1979), and in these female versions of *Huis Clos*, truths are told and identities are found and explored. Women's relationships to their bodies and to images of femininity have been explored in Louise Page's *Tissue* (1978), a delicate time-tracing of a woman's responses to the knowledge that she has breast cancer, and in Gilly Fraser's *A Bit of Rough* (Soho Poly, 1977), a realistic short play in which a woman considers genital self-mutilation after being raped.

It should be clear that the feminine, the female, any one or any combination of the feminist dynamics can appear in any kind of play written in any kind of form. Understanding why any specific dynamic appears is a very complex process, which combines knowledge of what ideas are in the air, what the state of the nation is, what the state of theatre is, and what the particular history and interests and political (or anti-political) make-up each writer has. While it is possible to analyse a particular writer's work in terms of her preoccupations, her style, her ideas, it has to be remembered that the meanings of each play cannot simply be 'read off' from what a writer says about her work, although whatever she does say is bound to be interesting and illuminating. A writer may be a very articulate feminist in her own life, but not write overtly didactic plays; a writer may deny in real life that she has much connection with feminism, and yet she may 'pick up' and utilise in her work the kinds of polemic comments which might be more at home in a straightforward agitprop work. In any case, most writers are interested in a whole range of issues, and will write with different emphases at different times. This should not stop others trying to evaluate their work; it simply means that most of the time when someone reads a play, or sees a play, or is involved in producing it, they do not have the benefit of having the writer there to tell them what it should or might mean; they must discern and interpret from their own point of view.

It is always very important to analyse the relationship between form and content; but it is also important to keep the analysis as fluid as possible. From the very wide range of plays discussed in this book, it should be obvious that there is not much to be gained from assuming that drama is per se some kind of 'male form', and that when women write, they write in a totally different form which has never been invented before and which is common to women. Emotional, aesthetic and structural styles are very varied among women writers; what is powerfully and importantly new is the content, and this must not be underestimated. It is the combination of the content and the writer's approach to it which produces the form which she thinks or feels is most appropriate. In a play such as *Blood Relations* (British production in 1985) by Canadian writer Sharon Pollock, the stage action shifts from 'reality' in the surface narrative to a whole range of different levels of illusion, in keeping with the thriller conundrum of the subject matter – did Lizzie Borden kill her parents or didn't she? The form asks the audience these questions implicitly, while the content (conversations and conflicts between characters) explores the questions explicitly. Nell Dunn's play *Steaming*, produced as a successful comedy, might convey different meanings if it was produced as more of a 'straight' play. The women might convey different nuances of subtext if the way they presented their nudity onstage was less voyeuristic than the original production.

Michelene Wandor

To end this section on women writers, I have decided to write something about my own work. In the first version of this book I slipped in one or two references to my plays as part of the general discussion. Given that in writing this book I am wearing my critical hat, I was not quite sure whether it was ethically right, or simply false modesty, that I should keep my own plays in the shadow. So this time, both in order to counter the false modesty, but also for the historical record, I have decided to include myself – bearing in mind what I said above about not making crude assumptions that everything a writer says about her own work is necessarily accurate. It will, however, be as accurate as I can make it, given my own vested interests.

I began writing plays in 1969–70, which for me (as for many other people) was a time of great personal turmoil and political and theatrical excitement. I was writing and reading my own poetry, and was immediately and very enthusiastically involved with the new Women's Liberation Movement, reviewing theatre, books and films for *Time Out*, then a radical new cultural guide to London. My first plays were short, rather surreal little efforts: one called *Bragafruit* was about two kings (sic) who grow an apple and an orange; another was called *You Two Can be Ticklish* about a couple who hire a man from an agency and tickle him to death. I suppose in some kind of way I was beginning to think imaginatively about ideas of authority, and critiques of marriage. Both plays were put on in pub theatres in 1970. In 1971 *The Day After Yesterday* was produced; this was a play about two couples watching the 'Miss World' contest on television, demonstrating the hypocrisy of middle-class morality (I think). Looking back on it now, it was stylistically interesting in that the first section was cartoon-like, short, stylised scenes, and the second half one long, naturalistic scene.

Director Malcolm Griffiths came to see this play, and asked me to write two plays for Portable Theatre Workshop, which he was then running. The two plays, *Mal de Mère* and *Split Milk*, were done as part of a multi-writers' programme; all the others were men, and I met none of them. Portable Theatre Workshop (which was the tail end of the writers-run Portable Theatre) then changed its name to Paradise Foundry, and I wrote for them a full programme of short plays, *To Die Among Friends* (1974), of which *Mal de Mère* was the opener and, I think, the most successful. In the five plays, each a two-hander, I explored different kinds of gender relations: mother-daughter in *Mal de Mère*; two male schoolfriends in *Christmas*; fraught young heterosexuality in *Joey*; politicised marriage in *Pearls*; and an alternative political/psycho-analytical relationship between two women in *Swallows*. Of the five, *Pearls* has the most polemic in it, since it was explicitly about a couple trying to change their lives in response to feminism. The others are sometimes poetic, sometimes elliptical, as befits plays which are about states of consciousness as well as about states of being. I am very fond of these plays.

However, as I have described much earlier in the book, the first half of the 1970s was a time when the vanguard of political theatre was to be found in collectivist work, and in the suspicion and rejection of the 'individualist' roles of writer and director. This caused me some doubt and anguish. I was not prepared to change my life and join a group that was devoting twenty-six hours a day to political theatre; my two small children would have been out in the cold. I think also at some level that having begun to find different kinds of literary voice (through poetry, plays and jour-nalism), I was not about to submerge that; I decided to go back to university and do an MA in the sociology of literature. Part of my motivation was because I wanted to find out why it was that I wanted to write. Of course, that was a stupid reason to do an MA. You only find out what you enjoy about writing and why you do it through doing more and then thinking about it, not through academic study alone. I did get a lot from doing the MA, but found that during the two and a half years it took me (during which I earned my living from journalism) I could write very little fiction. I wrote only a few poems and no plays.

When I returned to writing plays in 1976 (in my head I had never been away) I found that the theatre people I knew had assumed I'd given up. That was a bit of a shock, since I'd always known I was going back. But it took a year to write my first play after that, and some time to get it put on. All the non-fiction, as well as the heady contact with the socialist and feminist theatre companies, had made me think that I 'ought' to try to write social realism. So I did. I wrote *The Old Wives' Tale*, which was turned down rather thoughtlessly, I thought, by both the Royal Court and the Bush, and was put on, in 1977, enlightenedly, I thought, by Verity Bargate, who was then running the Soho Poly Theatre in London. Verity's work at the Soho Poly created a vital outlet for new plays, and she was particularly supportive to women writers.

After *The Old Wives' Tale* three experiences of working with companies followed in 1977: I scripted a play based on Kleist's *Penthesilea* for a fringe group called Salt Theatre. They had improvised a lot and then found they did not know how to script their play. I was contacted and did a very rushed job, and the product was not really satisfactory for anyone. I then scripted *Care and Control* for Gay Sweatshop; the company had researched, improvised and devised a play about the State and child custody. They had evolved a two-style structure which I liked very much: the first half, the naturalistic stories of three couples; the second half, a stylised version of two custody cases. The personal-political approach was reflected in the structure, and the State's attitude to motherhood, feminism and lesbianism combined to make it a very challenging piece of work. I felt that in the end the second half was far more effective than the first half – I would like to have reduced the number of characters to four, but that was never a possibility, since the company was already employed and cast. Nevertheless, apart from this small aesthetic limitation, the play worked well and toured very successfully. That year I also worked with three other writers on Monstrous Regiment's first cabaret, *Floorshow*; it was a very mixed experience, since the company had not really worked out how they would deal with a collaboration between writers, and we, as writers, did not know one another and had no clear structure to offer either. In the event we all wrote material, and the company just chose what it liked best. That meant a rather alienated working relationship, since in a sense the writers were discarded once they had served their use, and one's satisfaction had to be gleaned on the basis of how much of one's material they had used. They used some of my jokes and eventually one song. I didn't think that was fair. But the company was in control and their decision was final.

That year was very busy, and involved some very interesting contact with companies. I found all the collaborations (even the frustrating ones) illuminating, and again it fed back into my interest in reconciling my personal literary desires with my commitment to the political theatre network. However, at the end of these collaborations it seemed to me that the only way it could work was if the power relations were very clearly outlined at the beginning: either the writer was servicing the company, and had to refer always to them, or the company was serving the writer's script. These would have to be the base lines, I felt, and it seemed to me that if you knew where you started from, then that actually opened up the way to very real collaboration, based on a clear understanding of who had final control over the script.

I also felt that the social realism of *The Old Wives' Tale* and of the first part of *Care and Control* simply did not give me enough job satisfaction in the act of writing, and also did not enable me to convey some of the things I wanted to write about. I did another social-realist comedy called *Scissors* (Almost Free, 1978) which was a sort of Jewish, family-political comedy – the first time I had written about being Jewish. But the next two plays were very different and very exciting to write. The first was *Whores D'Oeuvres* (1978) which I wrote for two women students of Malcolm Griffiths, who was then teaching at Trent Polytechnic. I had total freedom, and I took advantage of it. The play is about two prostitutes who are cast away on a raft in the Thames. The play alternates real, daytime scenes with dream scenes; it is both a story about the two women, and an exploration of the images, the violence and the ideas which are attached to the notion of prostitution. There was at the time a debate about prostitution among feminists, and one line was that prostitution was not only a job, just like any other, but that it was a good way to get money back from men.

That annoyed me, and I used the opportunity to write a play which tried to explore the way in which prostitution affected women's relationships towards other women, and sexual self-identity. The play was theatrically very demanding; I thought it worked as a play, and still think it is very interesting and unusual. In its attempt to convey the relationship between the economic, ideological and personal consequences of prostitution, I would claim it as a social-ist-feminist dynamic.

The other 'free' piece of work I did was to dramatise – not on commission – Elizabeth Barrett Browning's very long verse novel, *Aurora Leigh*.[6] I retained the blank verse form, and in the course of the dramatising process, wrote verse to match the original in both metre and style. The dynamic in this play – as it is in the original – is a straightforward, bourgeois feminist one: Aurora, penniless daughter of an aristocrat, refuses an arranged marriage with her wealthy cousin Romney because she wants to be independent and a writer. She becomes independent, successful as a writer, and befriends a working-class woman who has an illegitimate baby after being raped. Aurora then re-meets Romney; in the original he is blind (the Mr Rochester syndrome), and he and Aurora are reconciled, with her independence vindicated and highlighted by his blindness. It seemed to me that this extreme symbolism, necessary in the 1850s, was no longer so, and leaving Romney his sight was my only modification of the original. It also seemed to me that the bourgeois feminist dynamic was so mild that it would surely be acceptable to the BBC, or the National, or to the Royal Shakespeare Company, all of whom could, I felt, deal with the verse form more adequately than a fringe group. Well. The BBC director returned the play with a puzzled 'But this isn't a play, is it?'; the National Theatre contact said, 'It isn't exactly Pushkin, is it?' (to which the only straight answer was 'Of course not'); and the RSC held on to the play for two years and then returned it with no comment. In 1979 the fringe group Mrs Worthington's Daughters did the first production, after which the BBC director realised it would work, and a different National Theatre director read it again, this time with positive response, and the play was broadcast, and then done at the National as a Platform perform-ance in 1981.

In 1978 I had a go at a slightly different form, writing what was meant to be a sub-Ayckbournian comedy about two couples, one heterosexual, the other lesbian, both of whom wanted a baby, *AID Thy Neighbour*. The following year I adapted my radio play, *Correspondence*, about a divorced woman, for the stage, and in 1981 adapted *The Blind Goddess* by Ernst Toller for Red Ladder theatre company. Since then, apart from an unperformed, full-length play about nineteenth-century South Africa, most of my dramatic work has been for the radio, which has given me far more scope and freedom than I had been finding in the theatre. I hope that imbalance will be redressed soon, since radio and theatre each have their own specific advantages and excitements, and the vitality of effective theatre work is what makes it such a magnet for both writers and audiences.

12
Conclusions and the future

A few weeks have passed since I finished the last chapter. I have been putting off writing the concluding chapter, with some perfectly good reasons for procrastinating. But upon getting down to it, I realise that it is virtually an impossible chapter to write, since there are no final conclusions to be drawn. Or rather, there is one fundamental conclusion: that the area of theatrical history represented in this book demonstrates how varied, exciting, contentious and necessary sexual politics are to the development of a healthy theatre of the future. Such a conclusion cannot be 'final' in any sense, since there is no guarantee whatsoever that feminism and gay politics will continue to challenge received theatre practice.

This is no pessimistic comment, but one which recognises that a number of preconditions are necessary before we can be sure that the traditions described here will continue: the first is that for quite some time to come, in the theatre as well as in the rest of our society, political feminism will have to continue to be a questioning and creative presence. It is also clear that the continuation of the subsidised theatre on a scale commensurate with its demands will ensure a stable climate and performance circuit for radical voices in the theatre. Of course there will always be people with enthusiasm and energy to be theatrically defiant, and work for love rather than money, but this is a recipe for quick turnover and exhaustion, not for the presence of a radical force which will help transform the theatre.

More particularly, the groups and organisations which have been campaigning for improvements in the employment of women in the theatre will need to continue to demand and organise for a parity of employment for women across the board. It is only when women are present in significant numbers in all theatre roles, initiatory as well as interpretive, that we shall see a theatre which represents the concerns of all its audience, not just the experiences of one half being relayed to the other half.

Throughout this book (apart from the odd comment here and there) I have steadfastly avoided pinning down definitions of a 'feminist' theatre, let alone of a 'feminist' aesthetic, using instead the concept of different kinds of 'feminist dynamic'. The phrases 'feminist theatre' or 'feminist play' can be very useful as shorthand pointers to a certain kind of work, but they are inadequate as concepts to enable us to understand the depth and richness and complexity of the relationship between radical work by women and the theatre. Indeed, as concepts they can end up lamely covering everything done by or about women, and that simply isn't good enough. I hope that the analytical comments I have made about some plays will serve as indicators for people either to use for other plays, or as starting points for a way of looking at work by women which produces genuine understanding and illumination. In a sense every play, whether it is individually authored or group produced, needs to be stripped down to its various components before an analysis can be built up: taking into account the state of the nation, the state of the theatre, the context of that play's creation, production and distribution, the audiences to whom it plays, and the climate of response which it elicits.

This does not mean that I think that we should develop a calm and emotionless response to theatre; on the contrary. The great excitement about theatre is its live immediacy, the passions (expressed or not) aroused in its audiences, the responses ranging from the 'good night out' to the rage because one's consciousness has been assaulted, or the delight because one has recognised or empathised with something onstage, or because one is simply carried away by the excitement of the spectacle. Sexual politics enters a dangerous arena here because it touches on our most private and treasured views and feelings, and it is therefore bound to continue to be viewed with suspicion. But the very notion of dilemma, or conflict, or contradiction, is endemic to the very institution of theatre itself – the fundamental contradiction of the illusion in which we all collude – that some people are not what they seem and also far more than what they seem.

There can be no doubt at all that the past fifteen years have opened a new chapter in British theatrical history in terms of the representation of women and sexuality, and at my most optimistic I have no doubt at all that this tradition may well continue, if the preconditions already described are present. But it is worth bearing in mind that similar explosions of radicalism from women have faded in the past, and that means that the struggle to ensure the presence of women's theatrical voices will be continually felt. Feminism is still necessary; there is no such thing as 'post-feminism'; men can no longer claim to speak for women; hopefully the quality of men's own gender perceptions of themselves (whatever their sexual orientations) will appear more in plays by men than it has to date.

For women, meanwhile, there is virtually the whole of history to re-interpret from our point of view; there are a myriad theatre forms to work with, explore and transform; there is, above all, the challenge of excitement and debate about what we are doing, and about a history which demonstrates that the theatre needs sexual politics as excitingly as sexual politics needs the theatre.

Appendix: *All Het Up in Bradford*

The theatre group called the General Will had its heyday in the mid-1970s. It had its place in the political and cultural life of the town, and was a noted contributor to a wider movement in theatre.

The particular stimulus behind the General Will was the university. It had been quick off the mark when the explosion of new theatre occurred in the late 1960s, and a Fellow in Drama was employed to work with the students. A lot of new plays were performed (giving early opportunities to new writers). There was a high level of political debate in the university at the time – the International Socialists were coming on strong – and because of the close-knit nature of social and political life in the town, the university politics had its links with the Trades Council, the Communist Party, etc. Because everyone drank in the same pubs, lived in the same streets, there was none of the sense of isolation within one particular group that occurs in London – there was something of the lively interaction that must have been a feature of political organising and debating in the industrial towns during the nineteenth century. It was no coincidence, therefore, that once a group of people working from the university had produced a particular type of work (good, informative, funny and up to date agitprop) there should be a general response encouraging its continuation.

The style and practice of the General Will was quickly established. The work had an immediate, cartoon-strip flavour, rooted in music-hall knockabout, able to take a Marxist interpretation of events into Trades Clubs and union conferences as well as student refectories. It was sharp and witty and responded to events in a way which many later agitprop groups ceased to do. That was to happen to the General Will itself in time, and that failure to respond was to happen when Arts Council funding on an annual basis had been achieved. Forward planning of the type which bureaucracies demand does not allow for work that is responsive, which is able to take from the moment and create work that will intervene in a current debate, crisis or movement. When I first worked with the group, however (in 1973 I think), it was still poor enough to have control over its own creativity. We made a play about prisons and the law, working alongside people involved with PROP and RAP, which were flourishing at the time. A play which dealt with the issue from a radical perspective was definitely in order and we took it to prisoners' hostels, some borstals, conferences, meetings, as well as to students. It worked well at its grassroots level and did serve to develop the debates at the time. It was also polished and good 'theatre', with a shedding of the good-hearted roughness of the earlier work. We played in some studio theatres and Arts Centres, the Arts Council nodded approval and funding began to increase yearly.

Although the group continued with its newspaper-agitprop styles, other influences began to test the limits of that method. Feminism was beginning to challenge political groupings and organisations in the town, and radical gay politics was to follow close on its heels. The day of the 'objective' male appraisal of the world was over, and it was becoming clear that a strictly-applied Marxism was no longer going to be a mallet to whack us over the head and into line. The General Will struggled valiantly to respond to these deabtes, but it was on a losing wicket from the start, since it was composed mainly of men, all of whom were heterosexual apart from myself. There were attempts to incorporate more women into the group, and I got up the nerve to introduce a couple of gay songs into our cabaret show; but the more we attempted to reflect in our work the debates going on at pubs, parties and meetings, the more of a tangle we got into. Radical politics in the town had outstripped us. Meantime, the work was of a high standard and we were in receipt of a decent sum of money from the ACGB each year.

I now come to a difficult area to write about, because it involves the most painful rupture of friendships and relationships. To put it baldly, the only way out of the political cul-de-sac in which the General Will had found itself was to wipe the slate clean and start over; to reconstitute the group in a way that did reflect the radical politics every member of the group recognised, but which could not surface in the work. As is the case in such circumstances, personal grudges, political instincts and money collided in a very messy way, and although the outcome of the ensuing power struggle was, I believe, the right one, the unfolding of it was not easy. In essence, control of the General Will (that is, its resources, name and financial administration) was transferred to lesbians and gay men, and if I use the word 'forcefully', remember that this was the era of the political zap. The General Will was zapped.

The basic facts are that as the General Will lost the inside track in the developing radical politics in Bradford, radical lesbianism and gay male politics were opening up new debates. A town-based GLF became focal not only in the area of debating sexuality, but in vigorously making its presence known in local politics generally, particularly in anti-fascist work. Traditional Left groups and parties – IS, IMG, WRP, CP, etc. – could not turn a blind eye to this (again, the intimate nature of the town) yet could not deny that it was the lesbian and gay movement in the town, of all the radical groups, which had a large, active, working-class support. By this, I mean that the movement consisted largely of working-class women and men from Bradford. I stress this because, although it is true to say that many GLF groups were located in the university world, there were elements of the movement which did not revolve around a middle-class, educated milieu. Bradford GLF did begin at the university, but quickly transferred to the already established Gay Centre – the one local gay pub, thronged with lesbians and gay men who would never have trekked up the hill to the lecture rooms. This is where the GLF found its membership. It's amusing – in a wry sort of way – to look back at conversations with left politicos who talked of 'building a movement in The Class', and seeing the look of blank incomprehension when they were told: 'but that's what we are doing in the GLF'. Somehow, there was (and is) the inference that lesbian and gay equals middle-class, and the proposition that the GLF was working-class based seemed a contradiction in terms to many of those politicos. I remember one, who would come to the gay pub to sell a WRP paper. We told him that we would willingly buy it if he consented to offer our own magazine for sale at his branch meetings. The same uncomprehending stare.

I am not attempting to pretend that we 'higher-educated' members of the GLF abandoned our individual aspirations or drives. My own particular input was to help form our GLF Theatre Workshop, and in the spring of 1975, at a conference on psychiatric attitudes to homosexuality, a cast of some twenty-five local people presented a play called *All Het Up*. It was hugely successful and is certainly the best piece of 'community theatre' I have ever known. It opened up a great well of creativity in the town, and for me, still a member of the General Will, highlighted my own frustrations in the group. By day, I participated in the increasingly despondent discussion in the company as to which way to go (and use our grant); in the evenings I'd be discussing new projects with the GLF, which knew exactly which way it wished to go (on no cash). At the point of retreating from the group, it became blindingly obvious that lateral thinking provided the answer: the new movement in theatre in the town should have control of the General Will.

There was resistance to this, and looking back, the most interesting aspect of that was the quite general response of the Left groupings: anger. Years later, I was to hear that remarks such as 'The queers have taken over' had been bandied about, and certainly not just in Bradford. When the final 'zap' happened after a couple of months of stormy meetings (I stopped mid-performance at a benefit show we were doing for the IS, which was also packed with lesbians and gays, and made a public statement which was later reported front page in *Gay News*, in its usual chintzy way, as 'Gay Actor in Showbiz Row'!). When that happened, the 'radical Left' reacted rather similarly to those outraged audiences attending the first performances of Wagner's operas.

If I do seem to be indulging slightly in score-settling it is because there has been no public statement concerning the Left's response to this GLF takeover of one of its institutions. Talk of noisy, rowdy, undisciplined gays muscling in, yes. It was, in fact, a radical, working-class-based movement expressing confidently an understanding of what radical theatre should be. (I could not have expressed it like that at the time, when the events were highly charged with personality.)

As it happened, the new structure for the General Will was achieved. A policy was made whereby not only lesbians and gays had access to the resources of the company, but ethnic minorities, women's groups and young people. For about a couple of years there was a mini boom of work (plays, new writing, music, schools projects) coming directly from the town. The work had a rough, rumbustious quality (of the type which often, in the hands of 'professional' Left groups attempting to woo the working classes, can seem painfully strained).

The work was upfront, usually without being simplistic, and generally eschewed the slightly apologetic tone of much Left theatre. Some of the heterosexual men from the 'old' General Will came back to share their skills. The events had in fact cleared the log-jam which the company had been stuck in and, for myself, proved that 'community theatre' (with the overtones of jolly, vapid, knees-ups to keep the people happy) could also be radical theatre (whose practitioners were so often groups of graduates on a grant, descending with the message out of the night, then back to London in the Gulbenkian van). Those are stereotypes and I know there were/are all shades inbetween, but they bear a certain validity.

'The personal is the political' was the starting point of lesbian and gay politics, and for myself is the centre still. The creative energy released in Bradford for that short period came from precisely the fact that a mass of people who had begun to fight for their own sexuality, in a collective way through GLF, had come to see that the dimensions of oppression are not merely about what is done to us. They include what is said of us, what is not said of us, how we are ignored and how we are stereotyped. For a time, there was a radical movement (however fraught with mistakes and limitations) in Bradford where making plays, attempting new ways of relating, sitting down in the street to stop the NF, producing magazines and partying were all aspects of the same thing: an attempt to see a community life where the private and the public were not at odds with each other, where all activities were given meaning through each other.

Noel Greig (*Platform*, spring 1983)

Notes

Preface to the second edition

1 *Strike While the Iron is Hot*, ed. Michelene Wandor, Journeyman Press, 1980.

3 The first phase: 1969–73

1 *Strike While the Iron is Hot*, ed. Michelene Wandor, Journeyman Press, 1980.

4 The second phase: 1973–7

1 *Strike While the Iron is Hot*, ed. Michelene Wandor, Journeyman Press, 1980.
2 *Two Gay Sweatshop Plays*, Gay Men's Press, 1981.
3 *Strike While the Iron is Hot*, op. cit.

5 The third phase: from 1977

1 *Plays Introduction*, Faber, 1984.
2 *Plays by Women*, Vol. 3, ed. Michelene Wandor, Methuen, 1984.
3 *Two Gay Sweatshop Plays*, Gay Men's Press, 1981.
4 *Teendreams*, Methuen, 1980.
5 *Five Plays* by Michelene Wandor, Playbooks/Journeyman, 1984.
6 Complete survey published by the Conference of Women Directors and Administrators, 23 Geraldine Road, London SW18.
7 Drama, 1984/2, British Theatre Association, 9 Fitzroy Square, London W1.

6   The skilled process

1 See the Appendix for a fuller account of this event.

7   Finding a voice: women playwrights and theatre

1 Compiled by Catherine Itzin, John Offord, 1980.
2 *Plays by Women*, ed. Michelene Wandor, Vols 1, 2, 3 and 4, Methuen, 1982–5.

11   The fourth phase: women playwrights in the 1970s and early 1980s

1 Published by Methuen, 1982.
2 *Plays by Women*, Vol. 1, ed. Michelene Wandor, Methuen, 1982.
3 Published by Amber Lane Press, 1979.
4 *Plays by Women*, Vol. 3, ed. Michelene Wandor, Methuen, 1984.
5 *Plays by Women*, Vol. 4, ed. Michelene Wandor, Methuen, 1985.
6 *Plays by Women*, Vol. 1, *op. cit.*

Bibliography

For a fairly comprehensive idea of how many women are writing plays, I would urge the reader to get *The Directory of Playwrights, Directors, Designers* (ed. Catherine Itzin, John Offord). Here you will also find lists of their plays, published and unpublished. Also it is well worth checking Samuel French's plays catalogue, particularly for plays aimed at the amateur drama market. Otherwise Methuen and Faber are the major drama publishers, although some other publishers bring out the occasional play. This bibliography consists of anthologies of plays which are of relevance to the content of this book, books of history and criticism which cover some of the same areas, and bibliographies.

History and criticism

Ackroyd, Peter, *Dressing Up. Transvestism and Drag: the History of an Obsession*, Thames & Hudson, 1979.

Chinoy, Helen Krich and Jenkins, Linda Walsh (eds), *Women in American Theatre*, Crown Publishers Inc, 1981.

Craig, Sandy (ed.), *Dreams and Deconstructions: Alternative Theatre in Britain*, Amber Lane Press, 1980.

Duffy, Maureen, *The Passionate Shepherdess* (a biography of Aphra Behn), Avon Books, 1979.

Dyer, Richard (ed.), *Gays and Film*, British Film Institute, 1977.

French, Marilyn, *Shakespeare's Division of Experience*, Abacus, 1983.

Gilder, Rosamond, *Enter the Actress: the First Women in the Theatre*, Theatre Arts Books, 1931.

Holledge, Julie, *Innocent Flowers: Women in Edwardian Theatre*, Virago, 1981.

Jardine, Lisa, *Still Harping on Daughters: Women and Drama in the Age of Shakespeare*, Harvester Press, 1983.

Keyssar, Helene, *Feminist Theatre*, Macmillan, 1984.

Malpede, Karen, *Women in Theatre: Compassion and Hope*, Drama Book Publishers, 1983.

Wandor, Michelene, *Orlando's Children; Gender, Sexuality and the Family in Post-war British Plays*, Methuen, 1986.

Anthologies

Berman, Ed (ed.), *Homosexual Acts* (plays by Robert Patrick, Laurence Collinson, Alan Wakeman), ambiance/almost free playscripts, 1, Interaction, 1975.

Greig, Noel and Griffiths, Drew, *Two Gay Sweatshop Plays*, Gay Men's Press, 1981.

Hatch, James and Sullivan, Victoria (eds), *Plays by and about Women* (plays by Alice Gerstenberg, Lillian Hellman, Clare Boothe, Doris Lessing, Megan Terry, Natalia Ginzburg, Maureen Duffy, Alice Childress), Vintage, 1974.

Hoffman, William M. (ed.), *Gay Plays* (plays by Robert Patrick, Bill Solly and Donald Ward, Susan Miller, Lanford Wilson, Joe Orton, Jane Chambers, Frank Marcus, William M. Hoffman and Anthony Holland), Avon Books, 1979.

Miles, Julia (ed.), *The Women's Project* (plays by Joyce Aaron/Luna Tarlo, Kathleen Collins, Penelope Gilliatt, Rose Leiman Goldemberg, Lavonne Mueller, Phyllis Purscell, Joan Schenkar), Performing Arts Journal Publications and American Place Theatre, 1980.

Moore, Honor (ed.), *The New Women's Theatre* (plays by Corinne Jacker, Joanna Russ, Ursule Molinaro, Tina Howe, Honor Moore, Alice Childress, Ruth Wolff, Joanna Halpert Kraus, Myrna Lamb, Eve Merriam, Paula Wagner and Jack Hoffsiss), Vintage, 1977.

Morgan, Fidelis (ed.), *The Female Wits: Women Playwrights of the Restoration* (plays by Aphra Behn, Catherine Trotter, Mary Delarivierer Manley, Mary Pix, Susannah Centlivre), Virago, 1981.

Wandor, Michelene (ed.), *Strike While the Iron is Hot* (plays from Gay Sweatshop, Red Ladder, Women's Theatre Group), Journeyman Press, 1980.

Wandor, Michelene (ed.), *Plays by Women, Vol. 1* (plays by Caryl Churchill, Pam Gems, Louise Page, Michelene Wandor), Methuen, 1982. *Vol. 2* (plays by Maureen Duffy, Rose Leiman Goldemberg, Claire Luckham, Olwen Wymark), Methuen, 1983. *Vol. 3* (plays by Pam Gems, Debbie Horsfield, Sharon Pollock, Lou Wakefield and the Women's Theatre Group), Methuen, 1984. *Vol. 4* (plays by Grace Dayley, Caryl Churchill, Liz Lochhead, Alison Lyssa), Methuen, 1985.

Wilcox, Michael (ed.), *Gay Plays* (plays by Tom McClenaghan,

Mordaunt Shairp, Martin Sherman, Michael Wilcox), Methuen, 1984.

Bibliographies

Batchelor, Eleanor (ed.), *Plays by Women* (British, American) Womanbooks, New York, 1977.
Helbing, Terry (ed.), *Directory of Gay Plays*, JH Press, 1980.

Index

P. 27 photocopy & send to Billy

Twelve-Pound Look, The, 84
Tynan, Kenneth, 9–10

Unity Theatre, 2–3, 122

Vagina Rex and the Gas Oven,
  40–1
Venables, Clare, 109–10, 112–13
Victoria, Queen, 7
Vinegar Tom, 59–60, 63, 167,
  169–70
Voices, 61

Wakefield, Lou, 67
Wakeman, Alan, 53
Walker, Rob, 84
Walter, Harriet, 102–3
Wandor, Michelene, 12, 36–7, 44,
  48, 56–7, 76, 79, 84, 124, 178,
  185–90
Warm, 69
Weeks, Jeff, 17–18, 26
Weill, Kurt, 69
Wertenbaker, Timberlake, 66
Wesker, Arnold, 140, 145–8
What the Hell is She Doing Here?,
  68
Who Knows, 70
Whores D'Oeuvres, 188
Wibberley, Jane, 48
Wild Bunch, The, 66
Williams, Carol, 183
Wilson, Snoo, 153
Woman's Work is Never Done, A,
  43, 96, 151

Women in Entertainment, 88,
  92–3
Women in Violence, 85
Women Live, 90–3
women playwrights, 121–9,
  161–90; *see also by name*
Women's Company, The, 49–50,
  58, 161
Women's Liberation Movement,
  12–16, 40–1
Women's Project, 79–80
Women's Street Theatre Group,
  37–8, 77
Women's Theatre Festivals, 47–9,
  57
Women's Theatre Group (WTG),
  34, 47–9, 51–3, 58, 61–8,
  77–81, 99
Wood, Rony, 116
Wood, Victoria, 105, 179
Woolf, Virginia, 75, 165
work, 4–5
Work to Role, 52
Workers' Theatre Movement
  (WTM), 2
Working Women's Charter, 15, 87
writing for the theatre, 124–9, 184
Wymark, Olwen, 57, 178, 182
Wyre's Cross, 84–5

Yobbo Nowt, 152
Yoga Class, 74
York, Susanna, 86
You Two Can be Ticklish, 185

putative p. 155

tannoy p. 83

p. 85 Alison's House
Susan Glaspell
loosely based on
the story of
Emily Dickinson